THE PRECOLUMBIAN CHILD

Dr. Max Shein

M.D., F.A.A.P.

THE PRECOLUMBIAN CHILD

Translated from the Spanish by
MARINA CASTAÑEDA

Illustrations by
JORGE FLORES

LABYRINTHOS
1992

To ROSITA
for the stolen time

To DANIEL
and those who will come from
Esther, Janet, and Bathia

CONTENTS

Contents

ILLUSTRATIONS

FOREWORD

THE FACE OF A CHILD

Nobody can doubt that children exist. We see them teeming through the cities, well dressed, or indeed as beggars when they sell us chewing gum or lottery tickets; or we hear them cry—often in the offices of pediatricians, those perverse saints dedicated to inoculating the childhood population, thereby satisfying the sadistic instincts and sanitary dreams of all doctors!

But mostly throughout the world we are not interested in children, especially other peoples' children. We ignore them, seldom write for them, hardly make films to entertain them; the plays that open in children's theaters are often the same or display the same bombastic mediocrity.

Standing out from this barren emptiness is the bespectacled and playful figure of Dr. Max Shein, dedicated both to gathering children in his pediatrician's office and collecting flutes and all sorts of prehispanic musical instruments. Now he has written a splendid, detailed, and entertaining book on children in the precolumbian age, a book that must be added to his many other publications and seminars in the field of pediatrics.

This is an invaluable book. Firstly, because of its meticulous and abundant sum of information; secondly, thanks to its well reasoned and pertinent observations, the text fills a vast and inexplicable void, patiently describing the role played by children in the prehispanic world—a role supposedly fulfilled by the conventional "graffiti" with which certain walls of our cities have been covered in recent years.*

*Dr. Glantz refers to the practice, in Mexico City, of covering *slum* areas with government posters proclaiming "Children are the future of Mexico," "Children are the joy of life," but doing nothing to ease their poverty and improve their way of living.

Dr. Shein evokes that prehispanic world of children with respect and tenderness; it emerges, at once clearly and terrifyingly, in the verses dedicated to children, in the learning and customs taught them, in the softness with which they are addressed, and the harshness with which they are also sacrificed in honor of Tlaloc, bringing their parents to tears so that the god may shower the earth with his watery favors.

But that manifest cruelty, part of an ancient social and ethical system, could never compete with contemporaneous society's violence against its own offspring—those unfortunate children who roam the streets at very early ages, engaged in marginal trades, sleeping outdoors at the mercy of the elements and the authorities.

This must be emphasized: and Max does so, patiently and responsibly, as he reviews the principal sources in an orderly and consistent way. He compiles a wealth of information and restructures it in explanatory chapters that place children in their true light, opening up new vistas as he sifts through all the superfluous information and lays bare the essence of prehispanic education. Precolumbian educational institutions were a totality based upon a very special concept of the human being: that the perfect harmony of countenance and heart, joined and fully intermingled, will give birth to the sage.

From earliest infancy the child learns that his face must express without deviation the feelings that dwell within his heart. The prehispanic child learns to live without masks; his countenance reveals his innermost being. That harmony between being and seeming becomes manifest only after a long process of learning, within a social system that promotes it.

The child learns to conduct his feelings and bodily expression in unison; at the end of his education he becomes a mature man, "owner of a face and a heart." Miguel León-Portilla has explained this in his book, *Toltecayotl: Aspectos de la Cultura Náhuatl.* This tenet is highlighted in the compilation carried out by Shein who, delving into the sources and separating the wheat from the chaff, delivers the child in his historical dynamism—consistent and mature, able to become, through education, a "strong heart with a wise face." Education thus builds an appearance, that of wisdom—but such an appearance is also a being.

Perhaps this also applies to Dr. Shein, a pediatrician who has devoted decades to the care of children and who is not content to cure their bodies with medicines or injections of vaccines. His concern goes further, as is amply demonstrated by this study: it is not enough to cure the body alone; the body must function within a coherent social structure that is respectful of children. Without it, the body is overlaid with a mask and acquires a false countenance. Our precolumbian ancestors knew it well when they defined the "mature man":

[He who has] A heart firm as stone,
resistant as the trunk of a tree,
a wise countenance.
To be the owner of a face and a heart.

There are possibly few mature men; one would have to seek them out—like finding a needle in a haystack, just as Max Shein sought to find those fragments among the old texts that allowed him to recreate the child of antiquity, often buried among obscure data and always trodden under by adults preoccupied with problems of their own.

Max has a wise countenance, indeed.

Margo Glantz
Director, Department of Literature,
Ministry of Fine Arts, Mexico

INTRODUCTION

The idea for this book arose during a year's sabbatical, divided between my twin interests in pediatrics and anthropology, which I enjoyed in England and Israel.

During one of the many excursions that are the essence of any change in atmosphere or the search of new horizons, while visiting the Bodleian Library at Oxford University, I came upon the original Codex Mendoza, on display and open for view under the heading of children's education. Months later I was able to examine it in depth, thanks to the kindness of Dr. Bruce Barker-Benfield of the Library's Western Manuscripts Department.

The rest of the story is that of an obsession become reality: the coming together of my interests within a single goal—the study of the precolumbian child. My main objective was to compile the literature scattered in many places, while making pertinent clarifications and comments, but without going deeply into interpretations that would be the matter for another sort of book.

The bibliography I consulted, though extensive, centered mainly on the works of Friar Bernardino de Sahagún (the Florentine Codex, the *General History of the Things of New Spain* in the Codex Mendoza), and *El Primer Nueva Corónica y Buen Gobierno* of Felipe Guamán Poma de Ayala.

My thanks are expressed to Dr. Margo Glantz, a friend of many years—perhaps that is why she was as patient and kind with me as she was—for having read and criticized the original manuscript.

Finally—and the most difficult to express—my thanks to artist Jorge Flores who, with great patience, love, and skill did graphic interpretations of the Codex Mendoza and the drawings of Felipe Guamán Poma de Ayala, composing each picture as though it were a work of art in itself; for which he worked closely with me during the writing of this book.

Chapter I

PROLOGUE:

CHILDREN IN HISTORY

*The history of children is a night-
mare from which we have only
recently begun to awaken.* —De Mause

In writing a book of this nature it seemed essential to summarize briefly the history of children in different places and times, so as to have points of comparison with the history of the precolumbian child.

Though I have gleaned some knowledge of the history of childhood because of the nature of my profession, what I found in the literature as I delved into it more deeply could not but astonish me.

"The attitude of a people or nation toward its children has never been an indicator of progress," Estrellita Karsh has said.[1] The child, complains a twentieth-century historian, is a neglected factor in all the phases of human development.[2]

The conclusions of research into the history of childhood are depressing. They tell a tale of abuse from remote times up until the present. It is a history both painful and monotonous. In *The History of Childhood* by Lloyd De Mause,[3] a broad description of infanticide and abandonment, as well as terrifying discipline and sexual abuse of children, is presented.

Among primitive peoples, the care of children was completely neglected; and this negligence endures, even in highly civilized nations of our immediate past. It is literally true, as a pediatrician notes, that "among primitive races (in space) and ancient peoples (in time) the newborn was predestined for murder."[4] In primitive societies the struggle for existence prevailed: individuals were sacrificed for the tribe's "well-being," and the newborn infant, the "weakest configuration of human protoplasm," suffered the most.[5]

1

Fig. 1. Raphael's "The Triumph of Galatea"
(Villa della Farnesina, Rome).

Children, says De Mause, "went into the wall"—meaning that they were immured in buildings and doorways "to reinforce their structure," a common practice since the construction of the walls of Jericho, 7000 years before our own era. The practice was noted in Germany as late as 1843.[6]

Throughout our history children have been mutilated, tattooed, scarified on their faces and bodies; they endured deformations of the skull and extremities, and, to this day, are subjected to ritual operations on the genitals (circumcision, infibulation).

In his book *The Child in Human Progress* George Henry Payne was the first to examine the incidence of infanticide and brutality against children; he relates the murder of twins in Benin (Nigeria) because of a belief in superfetation—a second, later conception—as a result of adulterous intercourse. (This belief may have persisted among the Aztecs too; they disliked twins and invariably killed one of them.) Children born on unlucky days were also sacrificed, as well as those born with a pelvic presentation (buttocks first), with teeth visible, or other anomalies. In some cultures this also applied to children who sneezed shortly after birth.[7]

Female infants suffered an even worse fate than their male counterparts. Their routine sacrifice makes for some of the saddest pages in human history. Even among the Greeks and Romans, the murder of female children and the glorification of the masculine element point to a latent barbarism.[8] And the situation was not much fairer for males. We must not forget that the infantry in Greek armies (and is this not still the case?), the vanguard commonly decimated by the enemy, was composed of children and young boys.

The use of opiates to "calm" children can be found in the history of all peoples. We find instructions for their use since the Ebers papyrus, a sixteenth-century B.C. Egyptian medical treatise, and up to documents of the last century recording the annual importation into England of 200 pounds of opiates meant to induce sleep in children—a sleep from which they often did not awaken.[9]

The Renaissance, a period of great progress and discovery, was no different from earlier times in its contempt for children. French historian Philippe Ariès states that "the child was an insignificant and inconvenient *thing* in the course of living."

In Tudor England the child was still "salted, swaddled and tied" as in ancient times; even in paintings by the Renaissance masters we can detect their slight concern and interest in children. Michelangelo's "Sacred Family" portrays a Jesus child with secondary (mature) sexual characteristics, to be seen in his hair, muscles, and body shape. Raphael's "The Triumph of Galatea" represents "little angels" with all the anatomical features of adults (Fig. 1).

In "Las Meninas," Velázquez portrays Margarita, five years old, as a little adult, without a single childlike trait. Among writers, Montaigne[10] relates: "I have lost a few children with some sadness but not much sorrow"; he also states that ''children have no visible corporeal form, nor a mind.''

During the seventeenth century, in England's American colonies, half the children died because of a lack of hygiene and because of epidemics of the plague, cholera, and smallpox. Between 1669 and 1671, while diarrhea was killing 2000 children because of treatments that merely replicated the errors of antiquity, the century witnessed a renaissance in the field of medicine—for adults. It is no wonder that William Penn should have complained thus about his contemporaries: ''They are more concerned with caring for their animals than for their children.''[11]

Eastern civilizations are no exception. In China, India, and Japan infanticide, especially of females, was deemed to be of divine origin. In China, during the reign of Tsin Chi Hoang (232 B.C.), wars and hunger led to the abandonment and drowning of girls in lovely urns; not until the time of Choen Tche (1633-62 A.D.) do we find the first official document against infanticide (1659):[12]

> I have heard the sad lament of girls submerged in urns filled with water to drown them; it is inexpressible . . . that the heart of a father or mother should be so cruel.

Of course, despite all of the above, there are also in the literature pages full of love for children, as when Minerva deflects the arrow aimed at Menelaos ''as a mother shoos away a fly when her son lies in a sweet slumber''; or the Talmudic ritual that greets the newborn as a blessing come to earth, and the planting of a cedar upon the birth of a boy or a pine upon that of a girl.[13]

May this summary serve as an introduction to our study of the child in the precolumbian world, so we may then compare the history of its children with what has been related so far.

Chapter II

THE PRECOLUMBIAN WORLD

In one of his latest books René Dubos presents an ingenious description of the precolumbian world; he explains the cultural diversity and the different locations of human settlements based, not only upon biological determinism, but also on the social variety of human beings, thus implying both freedom of choice and the intentionality of behavior.

As Dubos explains, man arrived upon the American continent between 20,000 and 50,000 years before our era. Yet indigenous social patterns were extremely varied. The first settlers from Asia brought a basically Stone-Age culture and the use of fire. Some tribes eventually learned to work metals, but other groups never went beyond stone weapons and tools. No American indigenous people discovered the plow or the wheel, and there were so many languages that tribes separated by only a few miles could hardly understand one another.

Dubos notes that great civilizations evolved in the Valley of Mexico, Central America, and in the highlands of Peru—but there was no equivalent of the Aztecs, Mayas, and Incas in the vast territories of present-day Canada and the United States. Populations in North America would reach only one million in 1492, compared with 15 million in Mesoamerica* and South America.[14]

*The region called Mesoamerica, from the point of view of cultural anthropology—not geography—is limited to the north in Mexico by the Pánuco River in the east and the Sinaloa River in the west; and to the south by a line that goes from the mouth of the Motagua River in the Gulf of Honduras to the Gulf of Nicoya, crossing Honduras and Nicaragua.

Universal usage divides the precolumbian history of Mesoamerica into cultural periods, each with its own basic and characteristic traits: the Prehistoric, the Archaic, the Preclassical, the Classical, the Postclassical, and the Historical.

The *Prehistoric period* begins with the arrival of the first settlers from Asia, devoted to hunting and gathering, ending around the year 3000 B.C. The *Archaic period* begins with the appearance of farming, pottery, the first villages, and a primitive social organization (3000 to 1800 B.C.).

The *Preclassic period* stretches from the end of the former period to the establishment of large indigenous centers; there is a greater cultural development (1800 to 100 B.C.), whose main exponents were the Olmecs.

The *Classical period*, lasting about 900 years (100 B.C. to 850 A.D.), witnesses the flourishing of the great cultures of Teotihuacán, in the Valley of Mexico, Monte Albán, in Oaxaca, and the first blossoming of the Maya, in Yucatan, and the cultures of Mexico's Pacific coast.

The *Postclassic period* proceeds from the years 850 to 1250 A.D., when Tenochtitlán is founded; the theocratic societies give way to militaristic ones.

The *Historic period*, from 1250 to 1521, ends with the conquest of Mexico and Peru; it is characterized by Aztec and Inca hegemony, that is, by the establishment of genuine governmental states, arising from numerous conquests and the subsequent tribute required of subjected peoples.[15]

In Peru, the cultural periods are very similar. The *Prehistoric* one, first, begins around 8000 B.C.; to the Asian migrations one would have to add the Polynesian migrations toward Peru, as many anthropologists have insisted, because of the undeniable similarity of cultural characteristics among America, Polynesia, and Melanesia. There were probably occasional transpacific contacts, but their effect on American culture was but slight. This period would include a Pre-Agricultural phase of hunting and gathering (8000 to 2500 B.C.), and an Ancient Agricultural phase, in which pottery had not yet made its appearance (2550 to 1250 B.C.).

The *Formative period*, from 1250 to 850 B.C., in which utilitarian pottery appears in the *Guañape* style.

Later, the period termed *Cultist* appears, from 850 to 500 B.C., whose main exponent is the *Chavín* culture.

The next period is the so-called *Experimental* one, from 500 to 300 B.C. (Paracas), which leads to the *Flowering* period, from 300 B.C. to 500 A.D. (Mochica-Nazca).

The *Middle* or *Expansionist period*, from 500 to 1000 A.D. (Tiahuanaco), followed by the *Middle Recent* or *Urbanistic period*, from 1000 to 1440 A.D. (Chimú).

Finally, the *Recent* or *Imperialistic period*, from 1440 to 1532 A.D., from the Incas until the Spanish conquest.[16]

A cursory analysis shows that the Mesoamerican Classical period coincides with the so-called Flowering period of Peru; the Mesoamerican Postclassic period with the Expansionist one of Tiahuanaco, and the two more recent, historical ones with the hegemony of the Aztecs in Mesoamerica and the Incas in South America.

Without following the above-mentioned chronological sequence—since the purpose of this chapter is not to review the history of all the peoples of the New World, but rather to present an idea of the most important precolumbian cultures in order to locate our subject matter of children in space and time—I will now go on to the major civilizations. These are the Aztecs, Mayas, and Incas, and I will summarize the precedents of their pre-Classical ancestors, like the Toltecs and other previous peoples, in the case of the Aztecs and Mayas, and the Mochicas and Chimús, in the case of the Incas.

The Aztecs

Aztec history can only be understood in the light of that tribe's difficult process of adaptation to an arid ecology, with severe limitations in arable land and no beasts of burden, aside from their struggles against hostile neighbors.

Perhaps the Aztecs' most important quality was the capacity for cultural absorption, which allowed them—often by distorting history—to appropriate the cultural achievements of all the precolumbian peoples that preceded them, and especially those of the Toltecs, who constituted the first civilization in the Valley of Mexico.

Thus did they appropriate the cultivation of corn, which became their main staple, though its development was actually first undertaken by the Olmecs living in the low areas of the Gulf of Mexico, in what are now the states of Veracruz and Tabasco, during the first millennium B.C.

Through conquest the Aztecs absorbed the cultures of Southern Mexico: thus, the Zapotec civilization which evolved from 500 B.C. to 1496 A.D., from the mountains and valleys of Oaxaca to the beaches of the Pacific. From the Toltecs, a Náhuatl-speaking people like themselves, they learned the calendar founded upon an astronomical year of 365 days, which allowed them to forecast exactly the seasons of the year, and thus to develop definitive farming techniques for the cultivation of domesticated corn, kidney beans, and chiles, while developing the use of cotton textiles.

From the Toltecs, who were skilled mechanics and brilliant architects, they also learned to build, using adobe bricks, stone, and cement. They probably played a role in the destruction of the Toltecs' political capital, the ancient Tollán (Tula), built in 900 A.D., some 50 miles to the north of ancient Tenochtitlán.

Starting from the mythical Aztlán, and after passing through Tula, the Aztecs reach the shores of Lake Texcoco in 1265 A.D. According to legend their pilgrimage in search of a settling place comes to an end in 1325, when they see, upon an island in the lake, an eagle perched upon a prickly pear cactus, eating a snake—in fulfillment of an ancient prophecy.

In that place they built the first temple to their god and the first houses of Tenochtitlán—later Mexico City—dividing the zone into four districts: to the southwest, Mojotlán; to the southeast, Teopan; to the northwest, Cuepopan, and to the north, Aztacalco—areas that would soon be renamed by the Spaniards San Juan, San Pablo, Santa María la Redonda, and San Sebasitán, respectively.

The Aztecs survived for several generations upon that inhospitable island surrounded by swamps, building up their population, protected as vassals to the people of Azcapotzalco, to whom they provided mercenary assistance in their wars against neighboring Texcoco and Culhuacán. In 1427, during the reign of their fourth king, Itzcóatl, the Aztecs joined forces with their enemies from Texcoco and Tlacopan and vanquished Azcapotzalco, thus obtaining their independence.

In 1440, during the reign of their fifth ruler, Moctezuma Ilhuicamina, the Aztecs undertook an expansion throughout the Valley of Mexico and neighboring areas; they later conquered what are now the states of Puebla, Morelos, Guerrero, and Oaxaca. Under Axayácatl (1469), they consolidated their territorial gains and then, under their eighth monarch, Ahuitzótl (1486), also incorporated the Mayas and Zapotecs—though they were unable to conquer the area of Tlaxcala to the east and the Tarascan kingdom to the northwest.

Ahuitzótl, son of Moctezuma I, the most warlike and cruel of the Aztec rulers, ordered an extension of the Great Temple of Mexico City; in its inaugural ceremony 20,000 captives were reportedly sacrificed. Aztec hegemony over the greater part of the Mexican territory reached its peak during the reign of Moctezuma II, the ninth and last king (1502-1519), just before the Spanish conquest in 1519.

Land was divided into hereditary tribal lots, the so-called *calpulli* (from *calli*, house), consisting of groups of houses belonging to an extended family which had the use of the communally owned land. The *calpulli* was a social unit that was established for the benefit of the tribe; its members worked to preserve the community as a whole.

Land cultivation was expanded through artificial ''floating'' lots (*chinampas*) reclaimed from the lake. The economy was based upon the cultivation of corn, kidney beans, and chiles, aside from domestic animals (a species of turkey, the *huaxolotl*, and the *ixcuintli*, dog), fish, and various hunting products. All of this, along with the further produce and raw materials obtained from afar by the well organized merchant caste (*pochtecas*), made possible Tenochtitlán's high density of population, estimated by some at 250,000 inhabitants upon the arrival of the Spaniards.

Aztec religion centered upon Huitzilopochtli, god of war and symbol of the sun, reborn every day if fed with human blood. Thus the sacrifices, especially of war captives, and the ritual cannibalism. The Aztecs also incorporated the gods of other peoples, including Quetzalcoatl, the Toltecs' god of wisdom.

Aside from the solar calendar taken from the Toltecs, the Aztecs also used a religious calendar of 260 days, the *tonalpohualli*. Their mathematical system, like that of the Mayas, was based upon units of twenty. Their pictographic writing on vegetable paper and deerskin, employed to record historical events as well as the tribute imposed on other peoples, reached a high degree of perfection.

Aztec social organization consisted of a monarchy structured according to the *calpulli's* social stratification: the plebeian class (*macehuales*) consisted of painters (*tlacuilos*), farmers (*mayeques*), cargo bearers (*tamemes*), builders, jewelers, carpenters, and so on.

Tenochtitlán came to be the largest city of precolumbian America. Crisscrossed by three large avenues and an aqueduct, its great civic center included the main religious buildings and the nobles' palaces, as well as the House of Eagles of the military chiefs. Aside from the *calmécac* or advanced schools and the *tlacochcalli* (arsenals), the civic center also included dozens of small pyramids with temples at their top, as well as the public market (*tianguis*), the ball courts, and even a zoo.

The most important building was the Great Temple to Huitzilopochtli, with a square base of 80 x 100 meters, a height of 30 meters, and 114 steps to reach its upper platforms. The northern face, dedicated to the god Tlaloc, was painted white and blue; the southern face, that of Huitzilopochtli, was done in white and red. There were also other temples, currently being excavated and reconstituted by archaeological teams.

At the time of the Spanish conquest the Aztecs had appropriated the scientific and technological ideas of the American continent, though they never attained the excellence of the Mayas in mathematics, hieroglyphic writing, or architecture; nor did they achieve the Incas' brilliance in textiles, metallurgy, or pottery.[17]

The Mayas

Maya civilization extended over a large part of Mesoamerica, which in Mexico included the state of Yucatán and parts of the states of Veracruz and Tabasco, and covered the territory of Guatemala and part of Honduras. The climate and geography ranged from the mild highlands of Guatemala to calcareous soils fed only by underground rivers, with poor vegetation and limited fauna; but there were also zones of heavy rainfall and luxuriant vegetation.

In the *Formative period*—up to about 300 B.C.—the Mayas shared with other Mesoamerican peoples the cultivation of corn and the production of monochrome pottery. In the *Classical period* they computed the astronomical year of 365 days, began using hieroglyphic writing, and building the great ceremonial centers, such as Tikal and Uaxactún. Their history includes the so-called Mexican period, beginning in 987 A.D. after the fall of Tollán, capital of the Toltecs, who were dispersed throughout the Maya territory, introducing religious and architectural elements as well as arms.

It is believed that Quetzalcoatl—Kukulcán in Mayan—arrived in Yucatán and greatly influenced the development of the Maya centers of Chichén Itzá and Mayapán. Mayan was the main language in the area when the Spaniards arrived. Yucatán Mayan is still spoken today by two million people.

The Mayas were organized into family clans, settled in city-states, and governed by a noble class assisted by the religious hierarchy. Their slaves were war captives or criminals sentenced to slavery. Farmers worked the land, but they also participated in urban construction. There were also specialists in various trades.

For the Mayas, the cultivation of corn represented more than a simple means of procuring food: corn was a god, the very basis of life—the gods had actually fashioned man out of it. They also cultivated kidney beans and gourds, supplementing their vegetable diet with fowl (pheasants, chickens, and turkeys, among others). They also cultivated cotton.

In their religious centers the Maya built temples shaped like step pyramids, sometimes containing tombs. Their artists were outstanding in *al fresco* mural painting, lovely examples of which can be seen at Bonampak. Aside from the religious temples, they also erected other buildings: ball courts, astronomical observatories, and steam baths. Sewage systems have also been found, as at Palenque.

From the first, the Mayas identified their gods with the natural phenomena of the agricultural cycle. The world had been created by Hunabkú and his son Itzamná, god of the heavens. Ixchel, his wife, was goddess of the moon, pregnancy, and floods; an important sanctuary was built in her honor on the island of Cozumel. The Mayas used mutilation for religious purposes: they pierced the earlobes, lower extremities, and the penis. They also pierced the tongue and passed a string of thorns through the resulting orifice.

Sacrifice was a vital part of Maya ritual. They frequently practiced it upon a variety of animals, but the supreme sacrifice was that of human life. The victims of these rites were enemy soldiers and slaves, but also free-born children of both sexes; Landa attributes this last measure of equality to "the absence in them of sexual sin" (Chapter XI, below). Sacrificial scenes are clearly depicted in Maya sculpture, pottery, and murals; for them, as for the Aztecs, the practice derived from the belief that human blood was the essential food of the gods.

Like the Aztecs, the Mayas had a liturgical year aside from the astronomical one of 365 days—the *tzonkil* of 260 days, which regulated religious life. The computation of time was effected by using mathematical notation known to them from very early on: the numbers from one to twenty were represented by points and bars, where five points equalled one bar. The system was based upon the number of fingers and toes, what we call vigesimal.

The most important aspect of the Maya mathematical system was the assignment of a number's value according to its place in a sequence, but whereas in modern computation the digit to the left is ten times larger than its neighbor to the right, for the Mayas it was twenty times larger. They also had a symbol for the concept of zero.

The Mayas' greatest cultural achievement was their hieroglyphic writing, which consisted of a base sign accompanied by prefixes and suffixes modifying it. In some cases signs had a phonetic value; in others, they represented ideas—their definitive decipherment is only now beginning.[18]

The Incas

It was in the Andean region that the main South American civilizations developed, where different peoples gained hegemony, and great migratory movements took place. Around the year 2500 B.C. the first settlers appeared near the mouth of the Chicama River; they knew neither corn nor pottery.

Gradually, from about 1200 B.C., the foundations for future cultures were laid. In the northern Peruvian highlands to the east of the Blanca mountain range, the Chavín culture emerges with its typical feline god, introducing corn, and producing the first high quality *huacos* (pottery vessels). Metallurgy and weaving also began to develop.

Around 450 B.C., to the south of the Paracas region (150 miles to the south of Lima) a new culture flourished in a windy and desolate region; it produced ancient Peruvian weaving of excellent quality, often adorned with colorful bird feathers.

The Nazca culture blossomed from 400 B.C. to 1000 A.D. in southern Peru, between the basins of the Nazca and Ica rivers (200 to 300 miles to the south of Lima). Isolated by great deserts, its development was relatively independent. Nazca polychrome *huacos* are very beautiful and characteristic.

The Nazcas fell to the Chimús, as did the Mochicas. However, the flourishing of civilization in the northern valleys of the Peruvian coast included the Mochicas from 400 B.C. to 1000 A.D., and then the Chimús from 1000 to 1466.

From 400 B.C. to 1000 A.D. Mochica civilization developed on the northern coast of Peru, from the Huamy Valley (150 miles to the north of Lima) to the Leche River (500 miles to the north of Lima). Little is known of its early history; we now know more of its decadence after the Huari-Tiahuanaco invasion around 1000 A.D., when the entire Mochica area was absorbed by Chimú civilization.

In the year 1370 A.D. during the reign of Nanzenpinco, the Chimús completed their occupation of the coastal valleys and extended their domination, while preserving most of the Mochican culture. The land is extremely dry in this area because of its calcareous nature, the lack of rainfall, and the extreme heat, but the Mochicas solved the water problem with an elaborate system of irrigation canals, some of which were up to 60 miles long.

The Mochicas, Chimús, and other peoples of the coast all spoke Yunca, albeit with some differences from valley to valley; they had a tribal organization based on the *ayllú*—the basic social unit, of a collectivist nature, which has been defined as an extended family clan—in which land, animals, and crops belonged to the collective whole. The *ayllú* had a well defined territory; those living within it had access to whatever they needed.

Though these peoples worshiped the sun, like the Incas, the principal god of the Mochicas and Chimús was the moon, in whose honor they sacrificed children. They also worshiped water.

The Mochicas, more than any other precolumbian civilization, were outstanding in the manufacture of pottery. Their polychrome works—unlike the Chimús' black pottery—are unparalleled. They were generally made in molds by the women. Their great variety, and their depiction of animals and scenes from daily life fortunately compensate for the lack of other documentary evidence on Mochica life.

Their weaving was also of the highest quality, using cotton and wool made principally of alpaca and vicuña. As with the Aztecs, weaving with feathers was very common. Metallurgy was also a specialty of theirs from very early on; it would be improved upon by the Chumús.

All the civilizations of the Peruvian coasts and highlands were influenced by immigrants from the Tiahuanaco empire, beginning in 500 A.D. Their religious center was located at Tiahuanaco, near Lake Titicaca, 4000 meters above sea level, where one can still see great megalithic sculptures; their religious influence extended throughout all of Peru. Because of the climate, the main food in the area was the potato; the alpaca and the llama were the principal domestic animals.

Toward the middle of the fifteenth century these areas and civilizations were subjected by the Incas, who came from the Andean highlands near Cuzco to impose their language and lifestyle. Parting from a small territorial nucleus around primitive Cuzco, the Incas by the fifteenth century had built an empire extending from the Ancasmayo River (in today's Colombia) to the Maule River in Chile.

Little is known of the inhabitants of the Cuzco region before the appearance of the Incas in 1200 A.D. The early period of Inca history extends from that time until 1438.

Most chronicles agree on a succession of twelve rulers, beginning with the legendary Manco-Capac. But Inca civilization reached its greatest development from 1438 to 1471 under the rule of the ninth Pachacútec Inca Yupanqui, who undertook the territorial expansion that would be completed by his son Tupac Inca Yupanqui (1471 to 1493). With the fall of Chan-Chan, capital of the Chimú empire to the north, Inca territory extended over more than 2500 miles of Pacific coastline, reaching inland to the heights of the Andes.

The eleventh ruler, Huayna Capac, finished the subjugation of the inhabitants of a region stretching from Chile to Colombia. He was succeeded in 1525 by his son Huascar, but at the time of the Spaniards' arrival he was taken prisoner by his brother Atahualpa, who ordered his murder shortly before he himself was executed by the Spaniards.

The Incas imposed their language, Quechua, upon the subjugated peoples speaking Aymara or Yunca. Their social structure—taken from the peoples they conquered—was based on the *ayllú*, as described above.

The lowest class was made up of farmers, who cultivated corn, the potato, gourds, tomatoes, peanuts, manioc, and cotton. They knew quinine, an anti-malarial medicine, and coca, a narcotic plant whose anaesthetic alkaloid played an important role in ancient Peru. Domestic animals included rabbits, dogs, and ducks, which they ate, and llamas as beasts of burden. The farmers were called *puric*; they worked under foremen called *pachaca-curaca*; these in turn were supervised by local rulers (*honocuraca*), who answered to the governor of the province, who in turn obeyed the emperor *Sapa-Inca*.

The king was believed to be of divine origin, offspring of the sun; he thus had to marry another person of divine ascendance, generally his sister—though with a polygamous system he also could choose other women, sometimes hundreds of royal concubines.

Religion centered on the worship of natural phenomena. The principal god was the sun, followed by Viracocha, god of creation. The priests lived in temples and devoted themselves to the offering of sacrifices, which were human. The temple virgins prepared *chicha*, an alcoholic drink derived from fermented corn, and wove the king's clothes, made of alpaca wool.

The Incas never attained the Mochicas' excellence in pottery, but their accomplishments in engineering and architecture were exceptional. They built many suspension bridges over rivers as part of a unique communications system connecting Cuzco, their capital, with the most remote outposts of their territory.

The labor force for public works was provided by the *mita*, a mandatory public service imposed upon all inhabitants, as was military service.

Inca civilization, like its predecessors, also stands out for its textiles, probably the most delicate and beautiful of all the ancient peoples of America. Its metal-working skills in copper, silver, and gold were also unique.

The Incas had no writing system, not even pictographic, but they developed a very ingenius mnemotechnical method for counting and recording quantities on knotted ropes called *quipu*, which were the basis of the administrative system (Chapter VIII).

This summary, incomplete as it is, may give the reader a context within which to understand the role played by children in these societies, so different from those of Europe and Asia. They were cultures which, while still immersed in the stone age in some respects, mastered time and technology and created religions very different from those of the rest of the world.[19]

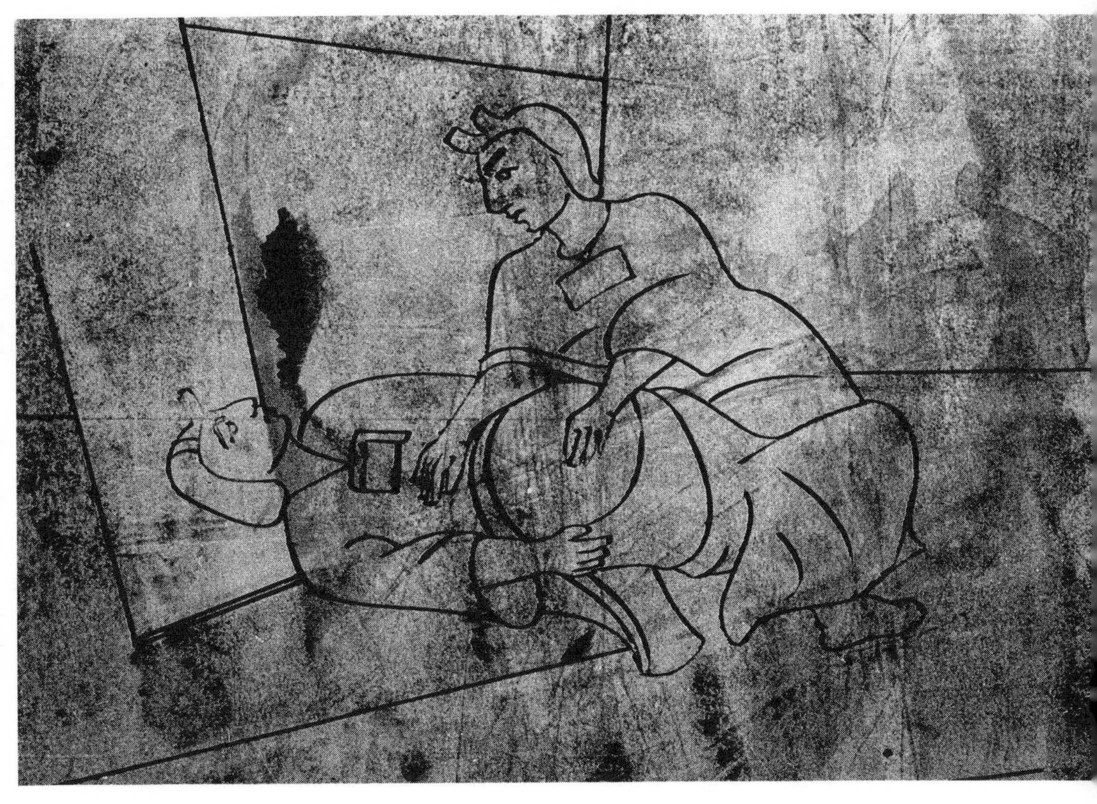

Fig. 2. Midwife (Florentine Codex).

Pilhuatia

Yo'om

---

*Chichu**

Chapter III

PREGNANCY

The midwife was an honored person,
worthy of veneration. . . .—Sahagún

Fray Bernardino de Sahagún† relates how the news of a pregnancy (*pilhuatia*) in a newly wedded woman was the occasion for great celebration. The two families would get together, inviting the village dignitaries, and "there was drinking, there was eating." They would then listen to the speech made by an elderly sage:

> And let those who are here, the old men, the old women, the white-haired ones, the white-headed ones, hear it! Our lord hath shown his mercy, our lord desireth now to show mercy to the girl, the child, the maiden, the newly wedded; he desireth to place within her a precious necklace, a precious feather; for the child hath conceived, hath become pregnant; for it seemeth that our lord desireth to place life within her. . . .[20]

The ceremony continued with congratulations offered by some other speaker, followed by a third on behalf of the father, who congratulates the pregnant woman, referring to her as "precious person, O precious bracelet. . . . Truly, now, we have acquired veritable wealth by virtue of our lord, for we have beheld in the coffer, in the reed chest, what we should not [otherwise] discern. . . .[21]

*Chapter titles are rendered here in Náhuatl, Mayan, and Quechua, respectively.
†Unless otherwise indicated in the references, all passages from Sahagún are taken from the Anderson and Dibble translation (see Bibliography).

Afterwards, the woman's parents answer the speeches, again referring to the baby as a precious stone and a wondrous feather. The final note of the ceremony is provided by the pregnant woman herself who wonders aloud whether she is worthy of bearing a child. Because of its beauty and humility I cite the response in its entirety:

My progenitors, my lords, precious persons, I have caused you to fall, to falter on the road; I have caused you torment. And ye know so much of our lord, ye know his secrets. No little thing have I caused you to forget, for already here I have rejoiced exceedingly, have enjoyed pleasure, for I have taken your motherhood, your fatherhood, the incomparable in your breasts, the wonderful, the precious.

Perhaps somewhere I shall reject them; perhaps somewhere there we shall reject them. For here, hearing them, is your humble one, the newly wedded. Our lord hath bound us together; he hath made us one. Who will so remember it? Verily, ye have grasped [the news], ye have received it; for in truth ye have heard that our lord inclineth his heart to grant such as is a precious necklace, a precious feather. Ah, verily, our lord wisheth to concede [the child]. Ah, it is said I have ruined my pregnancy. And behold, in what manner is our lord determining for me? Perhaps something is my desert [trial], my merit; perhaps the child will come to be born on earth; perhaps our lord will cause that with which I am adorned to see the light of day.

And here is thy humble one. Our hands are together; we go holding hands. Perhaps he will see, perhaps he will know, perhaps he will behold the face of what is his blood, his color, recognizable as his. Perhaps it will be his image. But on the other hand, the lord of the near, of the nigh, may laugh at us. Perhaps our lord will completely destroy the tender thing. Perhaps something will cause the baby, the tender thing, to sicken. Perhaps something will cause it to be stillborn; our lord will leave us [still] desiring a child.

Certainly we are weepers, we are sorrowers. Let us have faith in our lord; perhaps something is our desert, perhaps something is our merit. My progenitors, precious persons, my lords, find repose.[22]

When the pregnancy entered its seventh or eighth month, the families got together again, "and they drank, they ate," and chose the midwife who would attend the pregnant woman.[23] The midwife participated as minister in a religious cult closely linked to her medical function, and was referred to before the pregnant woman's relatives as a "precious person, our lady, noblewoman."[24]

With great respect they begged her to take charge of the pregnant woman, and, in a speech full of emotion, called her "very kind lady and spiritual mother," "the skilled one, the artisan of our lord."[25] The midwife's priestly

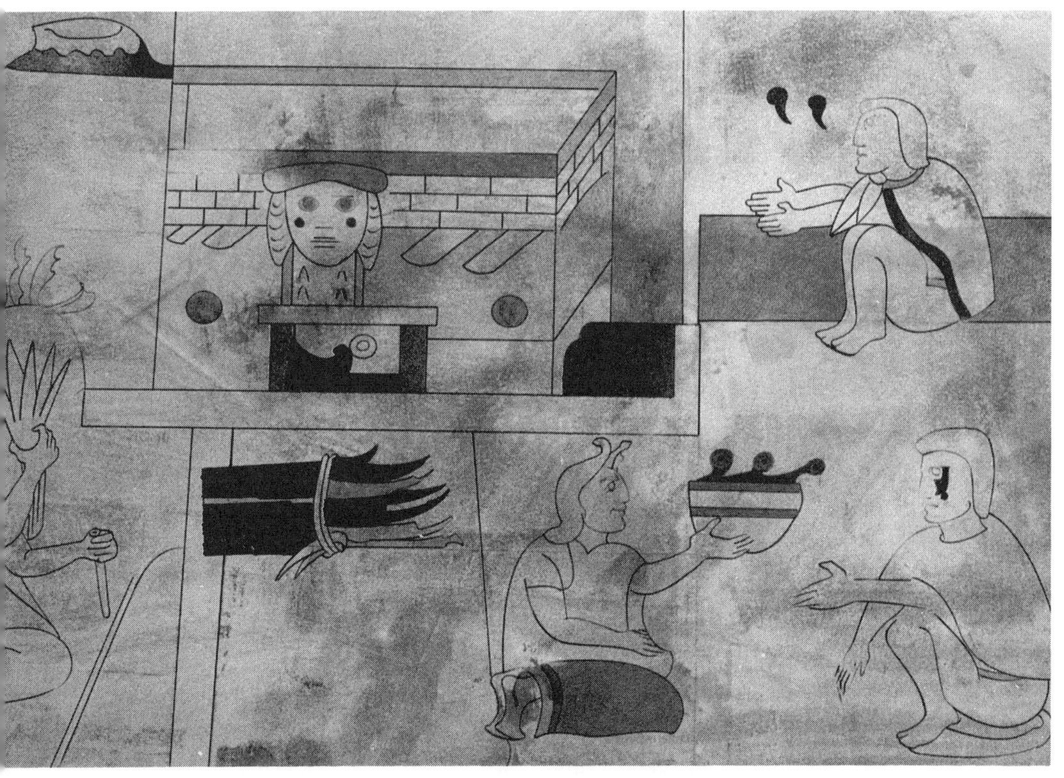

Fig. 3. Temazcal—sweat bath (Codex Magliabecchi).

character can be glimpsed in those words: it is also expressed in the ceremonies, in which she officiates during and after the birth, concerning both
mother and child.[26]

The pregnant woman was entrusted to the protection of the gods of gen-
eration and health, Teteoinan (mother of the gods and patron of midwives),
also called Temazcalteci ("grandmother of the sweatbath"—see Fig. 3) and
Ayopechtli or Ayopechcatl (a minor feminine deity who presided over
women's labor),[27] to whom there was a magical-religious invocation that
Sahagún left untranslated among his incantations to the gods, but which Angel
María Garibay has translated from the Náhuatl:

> In a place, in a place, in the house of Ayopechtli
> adorned with necklaces there is a giving birth.
> In a place, in a place, in the house of Ayopechtli
> adorned with necklaces there is a giving birth.
> In a place, in their house, ripened wombs are making life
> Rise up, come here; be the one who is sent,
> rise up, come here, new child!
> Rise up, come!
> Rise up, come; be the one who is sent
> rise up, come, jewel-child.
> rise up, come![28]

But Sahagún did not overlook the care given to the expectant mother:

> And at once, of her own accord, the midwife fired, [and] heated the
> sweatbath, and she put the maiden in the sweatbath, where she massaged
> the pregnant woman's abdomen; she placed [the unborn child] aright. She
> placed it straight; she kept turning it as she massaged her, as she went
> on manipulating her. But if the midwife was a little sick, some one of
> her representatives fired the sweatbath, to heat it. And when the pregnant
> woman came forth from the sweatbath, at that time she massaged her.
> [Fig. 2.]
> Many times the midwife massaged the abdomen of the pregnant wom-
> an. Sometimes it was even outside the sweatbath, nor was the pregnant
> woman [always] bathed in the sweatbath. It was said she just massaged
> her [until] raw. . . . Likewise, the midwife commanded that the pregnant
> woman should not become very hot, and her back should not be heated,
> either in the sun or at the fire, for her child would also roast. And the
> midwife commanded—sternly commanded—the pregnant woman not to
> sleep by day, for the child when born would be of abnormally large
> eyelids.
> Many were the commands that the midwife left to protect the pregnant
> woman, to provide her a particular mode of life all the time she was

pregnant. She said the pregnant woman should not chew chicle, for when the baby was born, its lips would be more than perforated; it would no more than nibble, since, it was said, its lips would be perforated, its lips would thicken. Since it could no longer suckle, it would die. She said it was necessary that she should look at nothing which angered one, which frightened one, which offended one, for she would bring the same [upon the child].

And what the pregnant woman desired should quickly be given; it should not be delayed; for her child would suffer if what she desired were not quickly given. And she said—she commanded—that she should not look upon anything red, for the child would be [extended] crosswise when it was to be born. And the midwife said that the pregnant woman should not fast, for it would cause the baby to starve. And she said the pregnant woman should not eat earth nor eat chalk, for the baby would not be born healthy; it would be restless; perhaps it would be sickly or perhaps not sound. For what the mother drank, what she ate, that also the baby absorbed; it took [substance] from her.[29]

The midwife also commanded the pregnant woman that "when what was within the pregnant woman was well formed, when it was already sound, when it was already great, no longer should she at any time take her pleasure with her husband, no longer should she give herself to worldliness, because the baby would not be born aright; it would come forth mingled with filth; as if bathed in white *atole* [cornflour gruel], . . . something rather shameful."[30] (It is curious to note that these last lines are omitted in the Spanish edition of Carlos María Bustamante, "out of decency, honor, and the respect I owe my readers.")[31]

There were many other superstitions: if the pregnant woman went out at night, she had to put ashes on her blouse or waist, so as not to be frightened by ghosts. If she looked at the sky during an eclipse her child would be born with a harelip, unless the mother had taken the precaution of wearing a knife underneath her clothing "next to the flesh."

If the father saw a ghost at night, it was said, the child would have a heart ailment. In sum, in the period preceding birth a whole set of traditional precepts and prohibitions enveloped the mother, and even the father, in order, as it was believed, to safeguard the child.[32] Other Aztec superstitions related to older children are recounted in Appendix A.

Throughout the pregnancy the role of the midwife was essential, especially with the young *ichpochpilhua* ("she who bears her first child").

Among the Mayas, marriage was undoubtedly an institution for procreation; they liked large families, which was perhaps an instinctive attitude in the face of very high mortality.[33] Women went on pilgrimages to the Island of Cozumel, to the temple of Ixchel, goddess of the moon and pregnancy, to plead for a fortunate birth. It was a dangerous sailing voyage of over 20 miles in fragile canoes, to cross the channel between the island and the Yucatán mainland. Sterile women also made the trip to pray for fertility.[34]

Among the Mayas it is cited that intercourse was not only permissible but "highly necessary during pregnancy," as it was believed that women needed the regular support of male semen for the child's proper development. They also thought the time of a child's conception would play a great role in his future life, and that certain unlucky days should be avoided.[35]

The history of pregnancy and childbirth among the Incas is very different from that of the Aztecs and Mayas. Many children were born and were also very well received, but the Incas did not have the midwives or preparatory rites that existed in Mexico.

For religious reasons pregnant women were not allowed to walk in the fields, and were obliged to confess their sins, to pray for a happy birth together with their husbands, and to fast during a brief period.[36]

There are few pages as full of tenderness, love, and respect for pregnant women as the ones cited at the beginning of this chapter—pages that bring to life magical-ritualistic practices and precepts not very different from those still subsisting in Mexico and other countries. Isn't an eclipse today as mysterious and charged with symbolism as it was in ancient times? Does not the modern husband go out of his way to fulfill the wishes or "cravings" of his expectant wife?

It is also obvious that precolumbian women, especially Aztecs, had rights and privileges that are reflected in the texts we have cited, and that their sexual function was highly valued by a warrior people for whom children were necessary and important.

Mixiuilztli

Kohol

Huachay

Chapter IV

CHILDBIRTH

*The midwife's knowledge and
technical skill were demonstrated
at the time of birth.* —Coury

The art of attending a birth—called ''the hour of death''—was highly developed among the Aztecs and probably among other precolumbian tribes, as is shown by similarities in the archaeological and pictographic evidence. The midwife's knowledge and technical skill were put to the test during delivery. Sahagún explains:

When the time of childbirth had arrived for the woman, then they summoned the midwife . . . perhaps yet four [or] five days before they were to give birth. They guarded them, they watched them periodically. And when she was to become aware of the labor pains, they said—it is said—they were to prepare food for her.

And when the woman already felt labor pains, in order that she would quickly give birth, they quickly bathed her in the sweat bath;* then they had her drink an [infusion of the root of an] herb named *cihuapatli*, an expellant, an ejectant. If the woman suffered much labor pain, they gave her as much as two fingers of opossum tail [ground up, in water] to drink, which would probably carry all with it. Thereby she quickly gave birth.[37]

*A feature of the *temazcalli*, bathhouse. The sweat- or steambath was a well established community practice in all Indian societies. (Codex Magliabecchi, folio 65.)

21

Fig. 4. Goddess giving birth, Mexica culture
(copy of the figurine, in the author's collection).

What implicit wisdom in the use of oxytocics, the medicines for speeding childbirth, like that obtained from the tail of the *tlacuache* (a Mexican marsupial, the opossum, *Diadelphis virginiana*)!

Sahagún's empirical observation that the meat and tail of this animal have such strong expelling properties involved a dog that secretly ate an entire opossum. "Such is the quality of the opossum that this dog came rejecting everything; it came casting everything out, defecating all its intestines."[38] Thus the dose of only half a finger of the animal's tail, because of its oxytocic and purgative qualities, was well calculated.

The infusion of the plant called *cihuapatli* ("woman's medicine," *Montanoa tomentosa*; "medicinal plant that has many species and whose boiled leaves are used in childbirth."—Siméon), cited in the Codex Badianus,[39] has unquestionable properties which, as Coury notes, have been experimentally proven.[40]

Childbirth generally took place in a genupectoral—squatting—position, the woman's weight on her heels. This position is reproduced in Maya figurines from Kaminaljuyú (Guatemala), in low reliefs from Sayil (Yucatán) and Monte Albán (Oaxaca), as well as many statuettes from Colima and Nayarit and various pictograms from ancient codices. Other examples have been found in Mochica pottery (Peru).

The most famous figurine of this type is undoubtedly the admirable statuette in the Robert Wood Bliss Collection of Dumbarton Oaks (Washington, D.C.), an extraordinarily realistic figure of a woman in labor, giving birth to a child who is emerging from her vagina (Fig. 4).

And (Sahagún continues) if problems arose during the delivery:

And if already in one day, one night, the woman could not give birth, then once again they quickly placed her in the sweatbath; once again they worked, and the midwife tried to straighten what was within the woman. And if she was despaired of, if she could in no way give birth to the baby, then they enclosed [isolated] the woman.

Only the midwife was by her [side], because she was offering prayers. She called upon, [and] prayed to Ciuacoatl, Quilaztli; then she cried out to Yoalticitl. . . . And the midwife who was prudent, who was skilled, if she saw that the baby had died, if it moved no more—and if the woman still lay gasping—then put her hand into the genitals of the woman. She inserted an obsidian knife; she dismembered the baby; she removed the body of the baby piece by piece.[41]

The midwives were evidently skilled at their job. If the child was badly positioned they carried out an external version, to change the position of the fetus by external manipulation on the abdominal wall. Nor did their knowledge end there: if the child died, they carried out an embryotomy *in utero* with a silex knife, to save the mother's life. "And if the parents dared not that the midwife do this [dismember the baby], then [the midwife] enclosed the little woman [without performing the embryotomy]. And if she died in childbirth, it is said she was named *mociuaquetzqui*.[42]

The *mociuaquetzqui*, "brave woman," who died in labor was the equivalent of soldiers who died in battle. Such women became goddesses and were called *cihuateteo* ("divine women"); their suffering and death were their apotheosis.[43] This divinization also took place among the Totonacs, the Mayas, and the Huastecs.[44]

Among precolumbian natives social and religious prestige was closely linked to procreation. Human reproduction was compared with the fertility of the soil. Many artistic representations have been found of pregnant women, or of childbirth, in Tlatilco, Nayarit, and Michoacán, as well as among the Gulf coast cultures, and in Costa Rica and Peru.[45]

For the Mayas, no single event was more important than the birth of a child. Children were not only considered a measure of personal wealth and good fortune, they were also seen as a blessing from the gods and especially from Ixchel, patroness of childbirth, whose image was placed beneath the mother's bed during labor, as is mentioned by Bishop Landa: "for childbirth they called upon a sorceress . . . and put underneath the bed an idol . . . by the name of Ixchel."[46]

Little is known of childbirth among the Mayas, though it can be inferred from customs among the Zinacantecs today that the mother was attended by a midwife (*x-alanzah*) assisted by the husband and several of his relatives, who drank intoxicating beverages during and after labor. The midwives foretold the day of birth and "facilitated" it, after which they used massage to return the uterus to its natural position.[47]

Among the Incas, the pregnant woman worked up to the very moment of birth, and delivery took place wherever she happened to be at the time. Sometimes she was helped by expert women neighbors, especially those who had given birth to twins. There were no professional midwives, and the mother herself cut the umbilical cord. Immediately after birth the mother would go to the nearest stream to bathe herself and the infant with water warmed in her own mouth; then she would place him in a cradle previously prepared (Fig. 21).[48]

Tlacatiliztli

Sih

Paccariy

Chapter V

BIRTH

. . . a place of thirst, a place of
hunger, a place of no gladness, a
place of no joy, a place of exhaustion,
of fatigue, of torment. —Sahagún

Among the Aztecs, at the moment of birth the midwife encouraged and stimulated the mother with shrill cries similar to those of a warrior in combat who had won a battle and gained a manly victory, having "captured a baby."[49]

The umbilical cord, *xicmetayotl* or "intestine of the umbilicus," was cut at a good distance from the child. Then the midwife spoke to the baby. If it was a male, she said: "Thou hast arrived on earth, my youngest one, my beloved boy, my beloved youth." If it was a female, she said, "Well beloved lady," and greeted her as a "precious stone and rich feather" in a long discourse in which she warned her of the uncertainty and hardship of life: "It becometh hot, it becometh cold, the wind bloweth. [It is] a place of thirst, a place of hunger, a place of no gladness, a place of no joy, a place of exhaustion, of fatigue, of torment. . . ."[50]

The umbilical cord had to be buried in a battlefield if the child was a boy, and in the home if it was a girl; thus, from the beginning, the man was destined to war and the woman to household duties. The burial of the cord "in the midst of a field given over to actions of war is a sign that you are offered and promised to the sun and the earth, is the sign of what you do in their profession. . . . [Y]ou must fulfill the office of war and your name will be inscribed upon the battlefield."

The girl's umbilical cord was buried in a corner of the house, and "this is a sign that the infant will not leave her home, will live in it as it is not fit that she go anywhere else; and this also signified that she should take care to prepare the family's food, drink, and clothing, and that her office was to know spinning and weaving.''

No description can equal the beauty of the original text cited by Sahagún, which I reproduce here almost in its entirety:

My precious son, my youngest one, behold the doctrine, the example which thy mother, thy father Yoaltecutli, Yoalticitl, have established. I take, I cut [the umbilical cord] from thy side, from thy middle.

Heed, hearken: thy home is not here, for thou art an eagle, thou art an ocelot; thou art a roseate spoonbill, thou art a troupial. Thou art the serpent, the bird of the lord of the near, of the nigh. Here is only the place of thy nest. Thou hast only been hatched here; thou hast only come, arrived. Thou art only come forth on earth here. Here dost thou bud, blossom, germinate. Here thou becomest the chip, the fragment [of thy mother]. Here are only thy cradle, thy cradle blanket, the resting place of thy head: only thy place of arrival.

Thou belongest out there; out there thou hast been consecrated. Thou hast been sent into warfare. War is thy desert, thy task. Thou shalt give drink, nourishment, food to the sun, the lord of the earth. Thy real home, thy property, thy lot is the home of the sun there in the heavens. Thou art to praise, to gladden Totonametlinmanye. Perhaps thou wilt receive the gift, perhaps thou wilt merit death by the obsidian knife, the flowered death by the obsidian knife.

And this which is lifted from thy side, which cometh from thy middle, I take from thee: the gift, the property of Tlaltecutli, Tonatiuh. And when war hath stirred, hath formed, it will be introduced into the hands of the eagle warriors, the ocelot warriors, the brave warriors. They go giving it to thy mother, thy father, Tonatiuh, Tlaltecutli; they go entering into the center, the middle, of the plains.

And thereby thou hast been assigned, thou hast been vowed to the sun, to Tlaltecutli; thereby thou deliverest thyself to him. And thus there within the battlefield thy name will be inscribed, will be registered in order that thy renown will not be forgotten, will not be lost. The precious thing removed from thy side is to be considered thy thorn, thy maguey, thy cane of tobacco, thy fir branch with which thou art to do penance, thy vow is to be fulfilled.

And now let us hope for something; perhaps we shall deserve, we shall merit something. Work, my precious son; may the lord of the near, of the nigh, yet give thee life, provide for thee, array thee.

And if it were a female, the midwife said to her, when she cut her umbilical cord:

My beloved maiden, my beloved noblewoman, thou hast endured fatigue! Our lord, the lord of the near, of the nigh, hath sent thee. Thou hast come to arrive at a place of weariness, a place of anguish, a place of fatigue where there is cold, there is wind.

And now take heed: from thy side, from thy middle I take it, I cut it [the umbilical cord]. Thy mother, thy father, Yoaltecutli, Yoalticitl, order it, request it. Thou wilt be in the heart of the home, thou wilt go nowhere, thou wilt nowhere become a wanderer, thou becomest the banked fire, the hearth stones. Here our lord planteth thee, burieth thee. And thou wilt become fatigued, thou wilt become tired; thou art to provide water, to grind maize, to drudge; thou art to sweat by the ashes, by the hearth. . . .

"Then," says Sahagún, "the midwife buried the umbilical cord of the noblewoman by the hearth. It was said that by this she signified that the little woman would nowhere wander. Her dwelling place was only within the house; her home was only within the house; it was not necessary for her to go anywhere. And it meant that her very duty was drink, food. She was to prepare drink, to prepare food, to grind, to spin, to weave."[51]

Afterwards, the midwife bathed the child while offering prayers to the goddess of water, Chalchiuhtlicue, so that water might wash away all traces of dirt, purifying and cleansing its heart and life. The birth was then announced to the family and neighborhood and, if it was a noble family, to the dignitaries of other cities. Then began a long ceremony in which many speakers came to greet the infant, who was again compared to precious jewels or lovely bird feathers. The family was praised and given presents, costly if the family was noble, or food and drink if they were *macehuales*.[52]

Francisco Clavijero recounts the ceremony of cutting the umbilical cord among the Mayas:[53]

. . . they would cut the umbilical cord upon an ear of corn, with a new knife which was then thrown into the river; they sowed the kernels from the corn and tended them as something sacred; from the resulting crop, they gave a part to the soothsayer, from another they made porridge for the infant, and stored the rest so the child could sow it when he was old enough to do so by himself. It was thus said that they ate not only from the sweat of their brows, but also from their very blood.

As has already been mentioned, the Incas had no special rites for birth. After cutting the cord and bathing the baby, the mother immediately returned to work. Yet birth was a welcome event and the woman who bore twins was elevated to sacred rank.

Fig. 5. Baptism (Codex Mendoza).

Chapter VI

BAPTISM

After the ceremonies described in the previous chapter, Aztec parents sent for a *tonalpouhqui* ("he who can discern the fortune of those who are born"), who consulted his book, the Tonalamatl, or book of destiny, to determine the sign of the child's birth to see if the day was propitious or unlucky. Four days later, the child was baptized; if the day of birth was unlucky, custom allowed for a religious fiction that postponed the ceremony until a more favorable date.[54]

In the third section of the Codex Mendoza we find an account of the ceremonial bath and baptism four days after a child's birth. It describes how[55]

> . . . the midwife took the naked baby in her arms and took it out to the courtyard of the mother's house . . . and the midwife bathed the creature . . . and at first when they took the baby out to bathe it, if it was a boy they put its insignia in its hand, and the insignia was the instrument with which the baby's father practiced his military art or a trade . . . and if the creature was a female the insignia with which they took her out to bathe was a distaff and spindle and a little basket and broom, the things she would practice when she reached the age. And the boy's umbilical cord, together with a shield and an arrow . . . was taken to the place where war was waged against enemies, and buried in the earth. . . . [T]he girl's umbilical cord was buried underneath the *metate*, a millstone used to grind cornmeal.

This was followed by a banquet at which guests strewed food and *pulque* upon the sacred fire, which had been lit since the beginning of labor as an offering to the ancient god of fire;[56] after the banquet the old men and women could devote themselves to the pleasure of drinking, after which the midwife gave the baby its name.

Boys were often named after the date of their birth: One cane, Two flower, Seven deer; or named after an animal, as in Nezahualcoyotl (hungry coyote); or named after a remembered forebear or some present-day event. Girls' names were based upon the word *xóchitl*, meaning flower; for instance, Matlalxóchitl (green flower), Quiauhxóchitl (rain flower).[57]

Citing Sahagún (Bk. VI, Ch. XXXVII), Soustelle describes with certain variations—while maintaining its essence—the ceremony of baptism with four rites of water, in which the midwife deposited a few drops of water in the child's mouth and said:

"See with what you will live upon the earth, so that you might grow and flourish, receive it." Then with her wet hand she touched the child's breast so as to cleanse and purify its heart.

Then she sprinkled several drops upon its head while reciting:

". . . receive and take the water of the lord of the world, that this clear blue celestial water might enter your body and live there."

And finally she washed the child's entire body while reciting a blessing to ward off all evil. After this, again four times, the midwife presented the child to the sky while invoking the sun.

Finally, she begged of the gods that the boy should be a valiant warrior. The last two parts of the ceremony were omitted for girls.[58]

The Codex Mendoza depicts these rites graphically (Fig. 5); the midwife carries the child and takes water for the ceremony from a jug. In the upper segment we can see the utensils and emblems used for boys: "weapons, arrows, and shields of extraordinary wood" (Solís, 1735); in the lower segment, those used for girls: spindle whorl, broom. Note also the footprints, suggesting that the baby was carried around the water jug while three children called out its given name.[59]

Among the Mayas, four or five days after its birth the child was taken to a priest for him to draw up its horoscope and predict even the profession it would follow as an adult. The priest also gave the child the name it would carry throughout its childhood, in a baptismal rite. A person's birthday was counted from the day of the *tzolkin* or sacred year in which he had been born, which also determined which gods would be favorable or unfavorable to the individual throughout his life.[60]

Friar Diego de Landa describes this visit as follows:[61]

> . . . at birth the children were bathed. . . . [T]hey were taken to the priest that he might tell their fortune and predict their profession and give them the name they would bear in the time of their childhood.[61]

Sylvanus Morley, making use of Ralph Royce's studies, calls this first name given a child at birth the *paal kaba* (literally, *kaba*, name, *paal*, childhood). For boys it invariably began with the prefix *Ah*; that of girls began with *Ix*. To these prefixes were added the names of mammals, reptiles, trees, or other natural objects: thus the boys were named Ah Balam (jaguar), Ah Ceh (deer), Ah Op (parrot), Ah Kutz (tobacco). Only a few feminine *paal* names have survived: they were formed by adding the feminine prefix *ix* to other Mayan words whose meanings are not as clear as that of the boys': Ix Chem, Ix Kahum, Ix Kan, Ix Kakuk.[62]

The second name give a child was that of the father. This name was taken soon after the ceremony for puberty, which will be described in a later chapter. We do not know the patronymic adolescents received when they were considered to have reached marriageable age.[63]

The third name given a person was that taken after marriage; it was called *naal kaba*, meaning maternal name in Mayan. It consisted of the prefix *Na* (mother), to which was added the mother's matronymic—that is, the mother's maiden name, followed by the father's patronymic or family name. Thus in the case of a man whose *naal* name was Na Chan Chel—the example used by Landa—the maiden name of the maternal grandmother was Chan, while the father's family name was Chel. This suggests that, if indeed the father's patronymic was transmitted to children for generations, so too the mother's matronymic was perpetuated for generations through her daughters.[64]

"Aside from the three types of names already mentioned, *paal* and *naal* and the father's patronymic," Morley continues, "there is a fourth that one of the indigenous manuscripts defines with the words *koko kaba* (nickname, humorous name). These names were probably given due to some individual peculiarity or circumstance, as in our 'Shorty' or 'Fats.' The six *koko kaba* that have survived in a manuscript are Ah Xun, Ah Pach Uitz, which might mean: 'the man who lives behind the hill;' Ah Tupp Kabal, possibly 'the man who makes a noise like an explosion;' Ah Na Itza, 'the man of the house of the Itzaes;' Ah Kom Tzohom, 'something red.' "

The *koko* name of Ah Zuitok Tutul Xiú, founder of Uxmal, was Hun Uitzil Chac, "the only mountain of Chac [god of rain]." The *koko* name of Hunac Ceel, whose victory in the struggle against Chac Xib Chac in 1194 put an end to the conferedation known as the League of Mayapán, was probably Ah Tapaynok, "he of the embroidered mantle." And, finally, Ah Xochil Ich, "owl face."[65]

Among the Incas, during his first years of life the child was simply called *huahua* (child). There were then two important ceremonies related to baptism. The first took place after weaning (between the ages of twelve and fourteen months); it marked his official entry into the *ayllú*.

It consisted of a simple ceremony in which a godfather, generally an elderly uncle, cut the infant's nails and hair with a silex knife. These were then kept by the family, as they were believed to have magical properties, along with the knife. During the ceremony the child was given a temporary name, generally related to the circumstances of his birth (fine sand, rain of oranges, closed fist, etc.).[66] The ceremony was called *rutu-chicoy*, which simply means haircut.[67]

The party was attended by all the child's relatives and some dignitaries, who drank and danced in great celebration; presents were given to the child and prayers offered to the sun that he might have a long and fruitful life.[68] Cieza de León relates that the ceremony took place fifteen to twenty days after birth.[69]

The child did not receive its definitive name until the second baptismal ceremony, at puberty, a ritual that will be described in Chapter VIII.

Piltzintli

———————

H'ch'o

———————

Huahua

Chapter VII

THE CHILD

Worthy of praise . . . was the
care in raising their children, . . .
taken by the Mexicans. —Acosta

"Nothing," relates Fray José de Acosta, "has surprised me more or seemed to me more worthy of praise and memory than the care and order in raising their children, taken by the Mexicans. Indeed, it would be difficult to find a nation which, at its noblest, should have been more diligent in this regard. . . ."[70]

All children were breast-fed; this was so generalized that "not even queens excused themselves, by their nobility, from feeding their children themselves," says Clavijero. If, due to illness or some other difficulty the mother was unable to fulfill this task, she did not entrust it to another woman before having "inspected the milk's fluidity upon her thumbnail."[71] "To see if it was good, she put some drops upon her nail; if it was sufficiently thick not to run, it was deemed good," runs another version.[72]

Alonso de Zorita was a keen reporter of domestic activities. "They cared for their diet by eating healthy meat and fruit."[73] "They are friends to their children, and raise them with such love that women, so as not to become pregnant while still breast-feeding, excuse themselves as much as possible from intercourse with their husbands; if they are widowed and are left with a child they are breast-feeding, they do not re-marry until they finish raising him; not to do so is seen as a great treason."[74]

As regards weaning, it is mentioned twice in the sources: Zorita[75] tells us it was done at age four and Vaillant[76] states that children were breast-fed until the age of three. Ablactation, that is, the introduction of non-milk foods into the diet, probably coincided with weaning.

33

Fig. 6. Straw crib, Mexica culture.

The baby was placed in a straw cradle with two big handles, as can be seen in the Codex Mendoza (Fig. 6), allowing the mother to move it at her convenience. Though there is no mention of a schedule for breast-feeding, it was probably done upon demand—that is, according to the baby's needs and rhythms. This can be deduced from the abundant love rhetoric addressed to children. As we shall see later on, this was not the case in South America's precolumbian cultures.

Children's education was of great concern to adults, among the Aztecs. It was carried out "with great solicitude and rigor," according to Clavijero. "From infancy they were accustomed to endure hunger, heat and cold; and from a young age they were instructed in the worship of the gods, and were taught the formulas to pray and implore protection, and were often taken to the temples so as to instill in them the love of religion, and small braziers were put in their cradles, offering up incense to the idols."[77]

Instruction began on the day of birth, with speeches by the parents and relatives predicting the child's destiny. Though they were considered small adults and citizens with full rights from the moment of birth, children were treated with considerable affection and were called "priceless jewels" or "precious feathers."[78]

Home education began after weaning, at the age of three or four. It sought to teach children the duties and techniques of adulthood as quickly as possible.[79] A world in which manual labor was common to all offered children opportunities for participation in adult activities much earlier than is the case, for instance, in our mechanized culture. Fathers oversaw the training of boys, while mothers instructed the girls.

Until the age of six they listened to frequently repeated homilies and advice, learned the use of domestic tools, and did domestic chores.[80]

Boys were given work as soon as they could walk; infants were made to carry small pieces of wood, whose weight was gradually augmented. They helped increasingly in chores around the home, carrying firewood and water, tending the fire and sweeping. The home education divided by the sexes continued: the father taught the son his duties, while the mother taught her daughter to grind corn, make *tortillas*, and weave clothing.

Aztec children were constantly urged on with long speeches regarding their destiny and their moral and ethical duties. Zorita quotes a speech given here in condensed form:

Reverence and health to your elders . . . console the poor . . . love, serve, and obey your parents. . . . Do not mock the elderly, the sick or deformed; humble yourself before the gods and hope that the same [infirmities] will not befall you. . . .

Be an honest and well-behaved son, be neither bothersome nor difficult with others, do not intrude where not invited . . . do not give a bad example or speak indiscreetly . . . do not get in the way. . . .[81]

An incredible speech, if we consider the historical period, in that it teaches children to respect adults, avoid evil, to seek truth and justice, obey authority, and even cultivate good manners!

An entire system of education based on oral tradition existed among the Náhuatl-speaking societies, and came to constitute a genre in itself. The first researchers called it *huehuetlatolli*, usually translated as "old folks' talk."[82]

Though there is no one work that fully encompasses this topic, "we are entitled," says the scholar Angel Garibay, "to establish the following postulates, which can be historically documented.

(A) From three to six years of age, the children were taken to the temples, in which there was a special hall for the teaching of myths, general morals, and rules for living together. These same types of teaching were to be found in the home, especially among the more important members of society.

Though collective education existed both for boys and girls, there was, especially for the girls, an on-going process of rehearsal at home. Sufficient information about these methods has come down to us in the surviving historical documents (see Appendices B and C).

(B) The teaching imparted in a group of educational establishments called *telpochcalli* ("house of young boys") was geared more toward action than thought. Yet, as a general rule, young people met daily from five to nine in the evening at the *cuicacalli* ("house of singing"). There they learned by heart the words and rhythms of religious or heroic chants, and practiced the steps of the various collective dances, which were the living and dramatic expression of their religious beliefs and what we would call their epic themes. It was as if they preserved in imagination the memory of events and situations which had helped shape their communities.

This is perfectly documented for Mexico and Texcoco, as well as Tlaxcala, Cholulá, and Cuauhtinchan. We have a good sampling of this sort of text in the known sources.

(C) Very different from these were other educational establishments: those called by the general name *calmécac* ("string of houses"), devoted to what we might term higher learning and which I will describe in a later chapter.[83]

At this point the research trail becomes easier to follow, thanks to the Codex Mendoza.[84] The Codex depicts a series of figures divided into two columns: one for boys, to the left, and one for girls, to the right. The two columns represent an account of the phases of development and home education in Aztec children. It also describes their food and clothing.

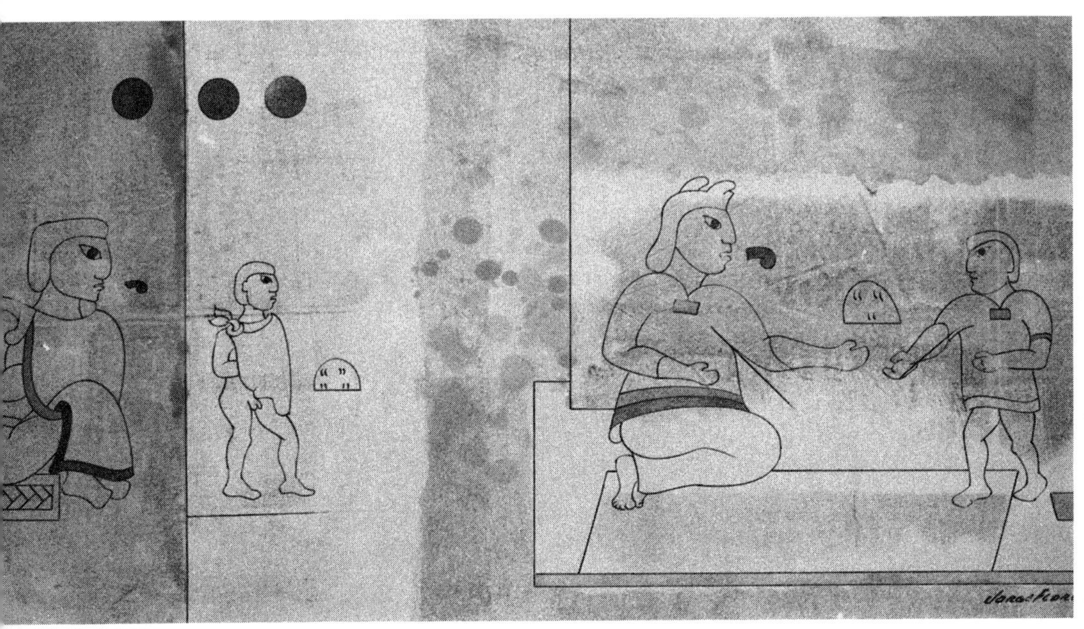

Fig. 7. Three-year-old children (Codex Mendoza).

Fig. 8. Four-year-old children (Codex Mendoza).

Fig. 9. Five-year-old children (Codex Mendoza).

Undoubtedly, the pictographic writing of the Codex Mendoza obeys certain conventions dictated by custom and religion; the *tlacuilo* (painter) entrusted with it followed the traditional norms in his drawings of Aztec symbolism. Despite this, the work has great artistic merit. And it has immense value as a historical document, as the drawings are accompanied by comments in Spanish based upon direct explanations of the manuscript's every detail.

The first page of the Codex was already described in the chapter on baptism. In this chapter we will describe folios 58, 59, and 60, which represent the life of children between the ages of three and fourteen years. Folio 58 has four parts, describing children of three, four, five, and six years.

In the strip devoted to three-year-olds (Fig. 7) we see on the boys' side, to the left, a father seated upon a straw bench with a blue rod (the color of precious stone) before his lips, because he is giving advice, explanations, and admonitions to the boy.

On the right side we see a mother who is entrusted with giving advice and admonitions to the daughter. At that age they are fed half a *tortilla* (know to measure about 9 inches in diameter) which, together with animal viscera (often kidneys), beans, and meat from the hunt, constituted a balanced and plentiful diet.

This strip, and probably the ensuing ones, refers to modest families; magistrates and important officials did not look after their children's education. We may also observe here the children's clothing, which consisted simply of a mantle tied upon the right shoulder, without the *maxtlatl* (a loincloth or wide band of cloth covering the genitals and reaching down to the thigh). The *maxtlatl* was used only after the age of thirteen.

Girls, from the beginning, wore blouses and short skirts that would grow progressively longer until they came down to the ankles.

In the following strip of folio 58 (Fig. 8) we see children at age four. Here, too, the father and mother appear with a blue rod before their lips, teaching the boy who is seen carrying water, while the girl observes the weaving utensils which her mother is evidently explaining to her. The food allowance has gone up to an entire *tortilla*.

In the next strip (Fig. 9), representing five-year-olds, the boy is seen carrying on his head and arms small boxes of firewood or bundles to take to the *tianguis* (or *tianquiztli*, market place). The girl observes her mother using the distaff and spindle. Both children continue to eat an entire *tortilla*.

The last strip on the same folio (Fig. 10) depicts children at age six, who are now eating a *tortilla* and a half. Following instructions given by the father, still with his rod, we see the boys collecting seeds and waste left on the *tianguis* grounds, whose pictogram also appears. The girl is already spinning beneath her mother's watchful eye and instructions. According to the Codex interpreter, such chores and occupations ''keep them busy, that they might not be idle, thus avoiding the evil vices that come from idleness.''

Folio 59, also in four strips, covers the ages of seven to ten years.

Fig. 10. Six-year-old children (Codex Mendoza).

Fig. 11. Seven-year-old children—punishment (Codex Mendoza).

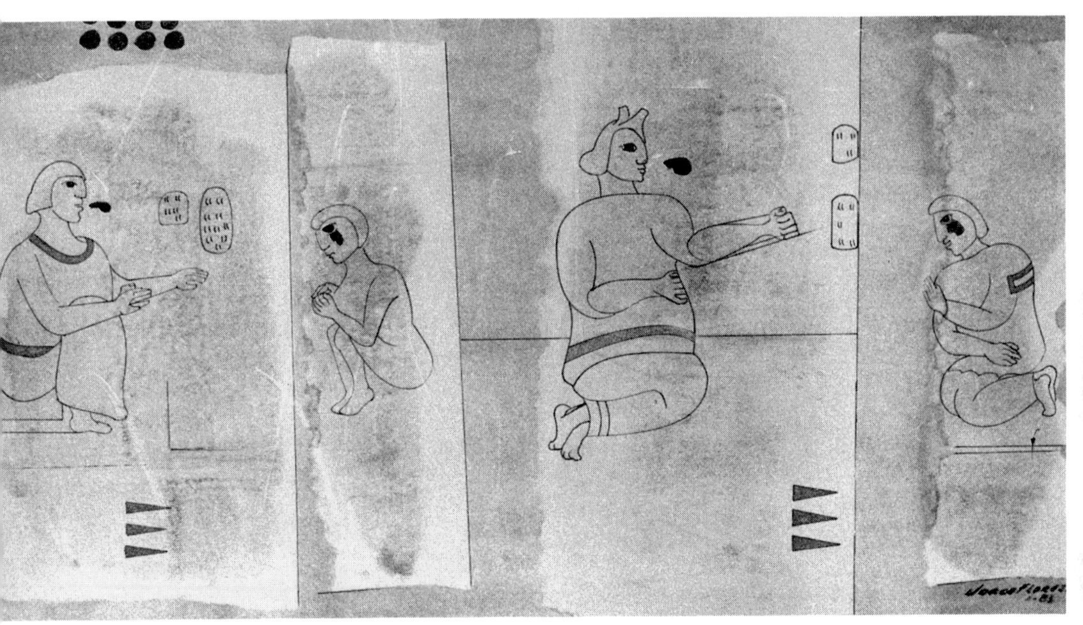

Fig. 12. Eight-year-old children—punishment (Codex Mendoza).

The first depicts children of seven years, whose food allowance still stands at one and a half *tortillas*. The corresponding text of the Codex Mendoza reads (Fig. 11):

> . . . in which parents instruct their children of seven years, giving the boys nets with which to fish, while mothers teach their daughters to spin and give them good advice to busy themselves always and spend the time in doing something so as to banish idleness.

The next three strips of this folio depict children eight, nine, and ten years of age. Their food ration continues to be one and a half *tortillas*. They depict the punishment given children who are lazy or have broken the rules. First they show them the thorns with which they will be punished; the children appear frightened and tearful (Fig. 12).

The next strip shows nine-year-old children (Fig. 13), who

> . . . for being disobedient and incorrigible are punished by their parents with thorns from the maguey cactus. The boy is tied hand and foot, naked, and is beaten with the thorns on his back and body; girls have their hands pricked with the thorns.

In the following strip (age ten—Fig. 14),

> . . . they are punished for being rebels, beating them with sticks and using other threats.

Folio 60 also contains four strips, covering ages eleven to fourteen. The first two strips also depict punishment (Fig. 15):

> The boys or girls of eleven years who do not mend their ways with words are punished by their parents, who make them inhale smoke with *axi* (chili), a grave and even cruel torment, so as to sicken them that they might leave their vicious and idle ways, applying themselves instead to spend the time in useful endeavors.

> As for the boys or girls of twelve years who refuse all correction and advice from their parents, the boy is taken by his father and tied hand and foot, naked, and stretched on the floor in a wet and humid place, and left there for an entire day, so that with this punishment he should be afraid. As for the girl, her mother makes her work at night [note the half-closed eyes in the pictogram between the two of them, signifying night], before daylight, having her sweep the house and street and always being occupied in chores. [Fig. 16]

Fig. 13. Nine-year-old children—punishment (Codex Mendoza).

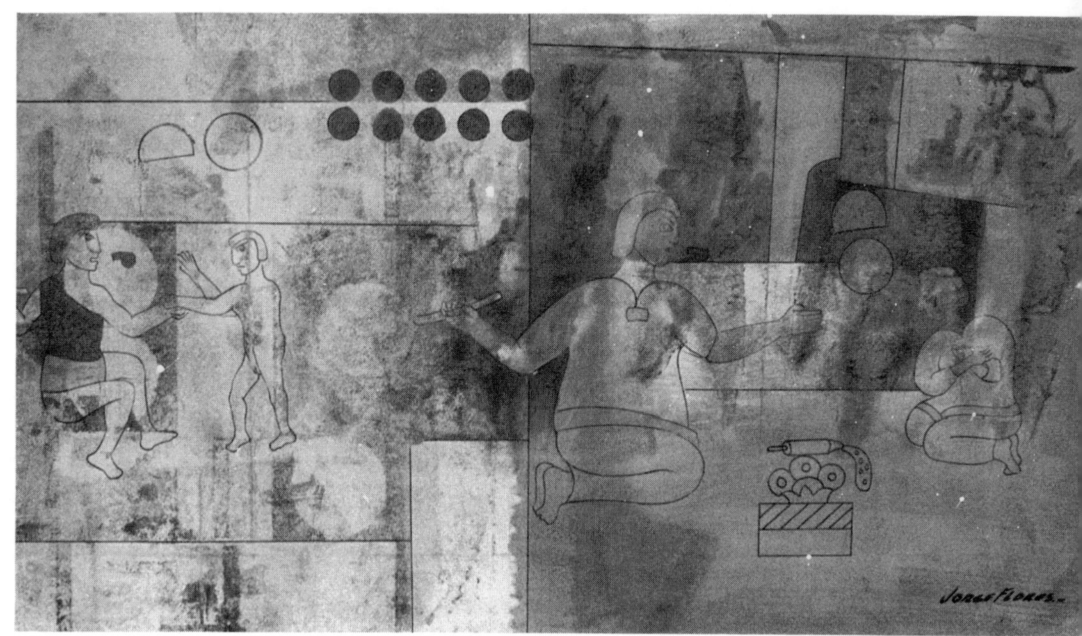

Fig. 14. Ten-year-old children—punishment (Codex Mendoza).

Fig. 15. Eleven-year-old children—punishment (Codex Mendoza).

Home education was undeniably practical and based on imitation. Regarding punishment, some authors state that the described severity was seldom applied; the descriptions in so many pictograms of the Codex are simply a result of Spaniards' questions asked of the *tlacuilo* about the punishment of children and do not reflect the true frequency or distribution of that activity.

Vaillant states that "until the age of eight, the principal means of discipline was admonition; from that age on, the obstinate child risked serious corporal punishment, but in view of the widespread tenderness indigenous parents show their children, these complicated punishments were probably but rarely applied."[85]

The third strip of folio 60 depicts children of thirteen:

> . . . parents make the boys bring firewood from the mountain, and reeds and other herbs for the household in canoes; [the girls] grind corn and make *tortillas* and other foods for their parents.

Children receive two *tortillas* each at every meal (Fig. 17).
At age fourteen (fourth strip of folio 60—Fig. 18):

> . . . their parents busy them, making the boys go fishing in the lagoons in a canoe, and the girls are made to weave any type of material for clothing.

So much for the Codex Mendoza's description of Aztec children and their domestic education!

Among the Mayas, Bishop Landa relates:[86]

> . . . that the Indian women raised their children with great harshness and nakedness, as four or five days after birth they put the child to lie on a small bed made of sticks, and there, face down, they put his head between two boards: one on the back of the head and the other on the forehead, between which they pressed the head tightly and had the creature suffering until a few days later its head was flat and molded the way they all had it.
>
> The hurt and danger to the poor children were such that some were in danger, and the author saw one's head perforated behind the ears, as must have happened to many. . . .

The methods used to deform the cranial cavity have been interpreted by different authors in various ways, as can be observed in Figs. 19 and 20; but the first seems to follow the description offered by Landa.

According to the Maya ideal of anatomical beauty, it was also highly desirable that the child should be strabismic, that is, cross-eyed; to this end,

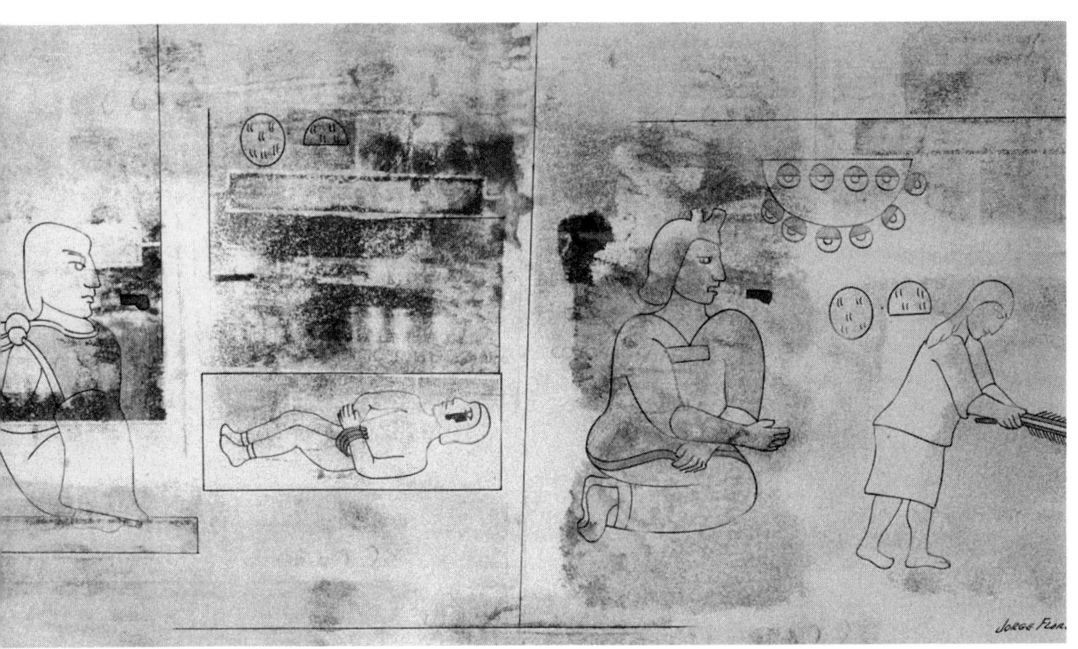

Fig. 16. Twelve-year-old children—punishment (Codex Mendoza).

Fig. 17. Thirteen-year-old children—punishment (Codex Mendoza).

Fig. 18. Fourteen-year-old children—punishment (Codex Mendoza).

his hair was tied in such a way that he would have, hanging between the eyes, a ball of resin and a small bright bead, to make the eyes focus inward (Fig. 20). The earlobes were pierced, as well as the nasal bone, the lips, and the nostrils, so as to accommodate a variety of ornaments.

At three or four months of age a ceremony called *hetzmek* took place, in which the child was set astride the hips of an adult chosen especially for the occasion. If it was a girl, this ceremony was done at three months, as three stones constitute the Maya hearth (*k'oben*), symbol of female occupations. If it was a boy, the ceremony took place at four months, as the earth in which corn is sown—symbol of men's work in the fields—has four corners.[87]

Godparents were generally chosen—a husband and wife—or a godfather for a boy and a godmother for a girl. The godparent then set the child astride his left hip, holding it with his left arm before a table on which were placed nine different objects that symbolized the child's future life. These the godfather placed one by one in the child's hands and, walking around the table, instructed him in their use.

The number of turns around the table was counted with kernels of corn placed among the other objects that were picked up after each turn. The godmother's turns were counted with gourd seeds; she ate one after each turn and then returned the child to its father, saying, "we have finished your son's *hetzmek*."

The father then knelt in gratitude, and later would feast the guests with abundant food and drink.[88] Nine is a lucky number among the Mayas, because it is associated with the nine steps leading to the ancient Maya paradise.[89]

"They were raised naked," says Morley, "except when, at age four or five, they were given a shawl to sleep on or some ribbons to cover their privates like their parents, and girls were covered from the waist down. They breast-fed in great quantity because they were given milk even at age three or four, which is why there were many strong people among them."[90]

"They grew wondrous lovely and fat in the first two years. Then, because they were continuously bathed by their mothers and the sun, they grew dark; but throughout their childhood they were pretty and playful, always going about with their bows and arrows and playing among themselves, and thus were they raised until they began to live as young people, becoming more aware of their manner and leaving behind the things of childhood."[91]

Most notations indicate that weaning, among the Mayas, took place around four years of age.[92] From an early age boys followed their fathers to the cornfields. Education was based on imitation, with knowledge following observation. Later on, they devoted themselves to hunting and learned from their fathers that absolutely everything in nature has a soul. Maya morals were based upon the group and upon cooperation; it was a great virtue to cooperate with the community.

Custom required that Mayas should be hospitable, offering their guests food and drink, and children were accustomed to take presents when they went

Fig. 19. Deformation of the cranial vault.

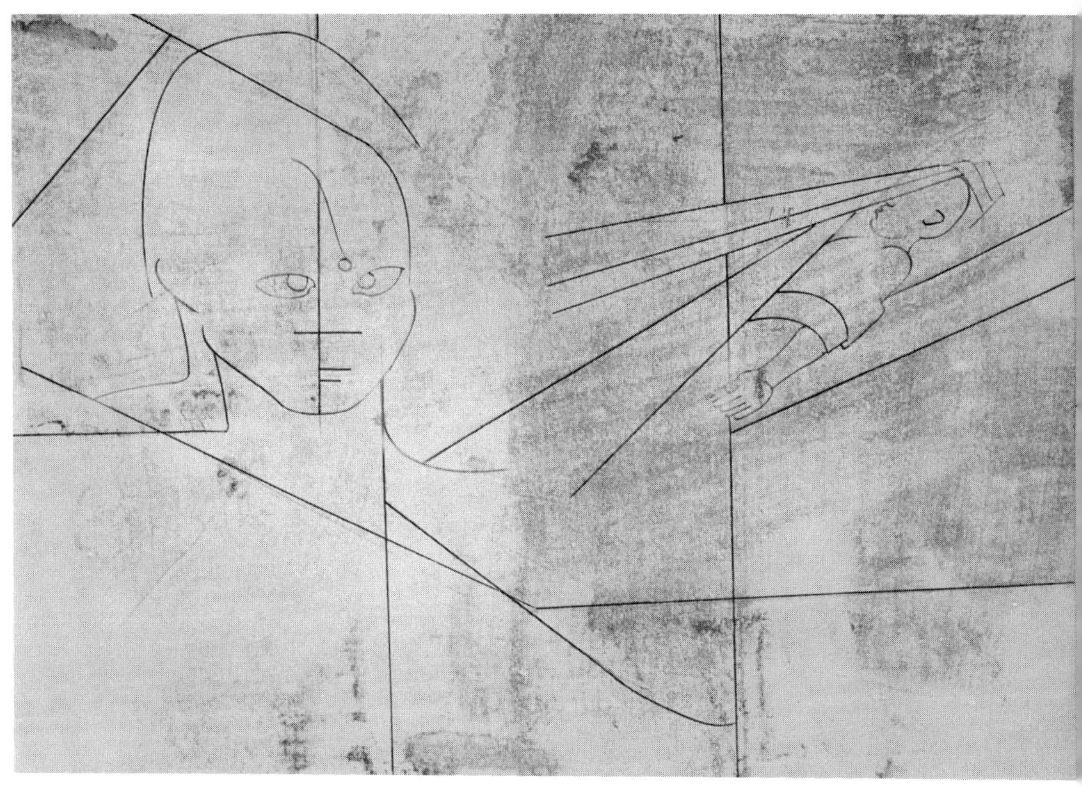

Fig. 20. Deformation of the cranial vault
and inducement of strabismus.

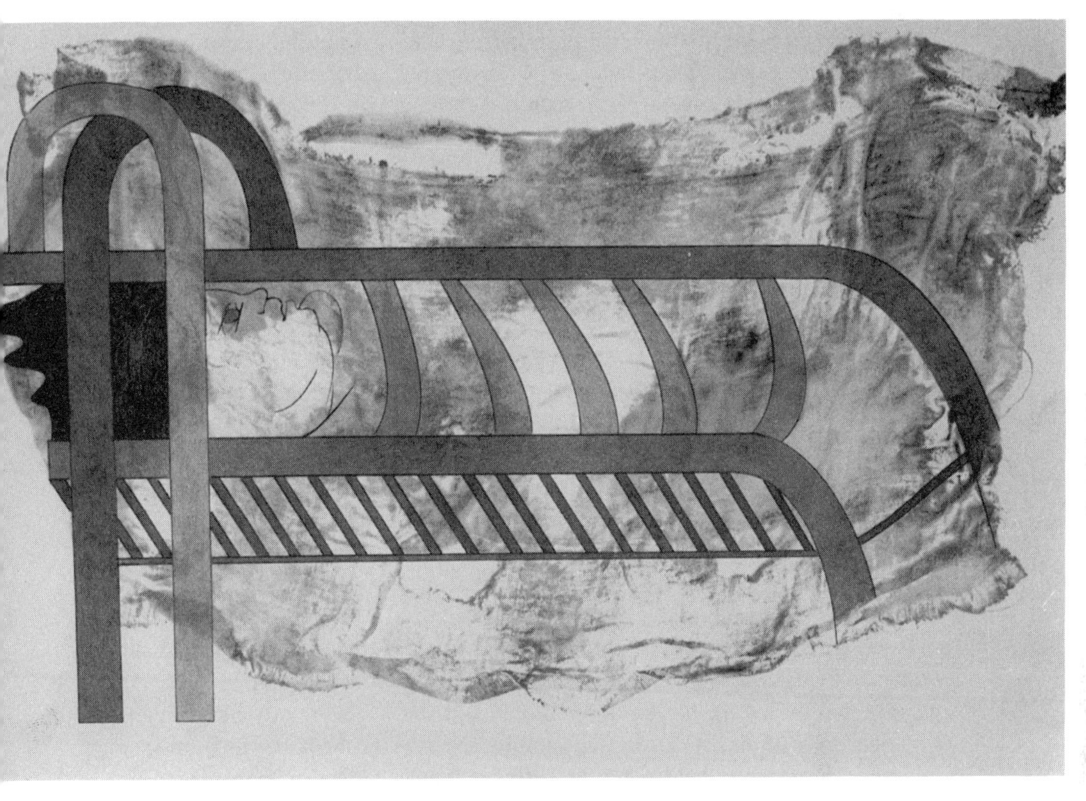

Fig. 21. Inca crib (Guamán Poma de Ayala).

visiting and to repeat the titles of persons on various occasions. They were also taught, when listening to someone speak, to emit a soft gutteral sound to show their interest and approval.[93]

Girls grew up in the image of their mothers, disciplined from the beginning, learning through rehearsal and repetition. They made *tortillas*, wove, spun, and learned by heart the prayers appropriate to their condition. As among the Aztecs, rhetoric was richly laden with advice and admonition; if they disobeyed, their earlobes were pricked until they bled, and if they relapsed their eyes were rubbed with hot peppers.[94]

When a boy reached the age of five a white bead was braided into his hair; girls at that age received a waistband with a red seashell, to be worn as a symbol of virginity. Neither object could be removed until an elaborate ritual had taken place to mark the beginning of adolescence, at age twelve in girls and fourteen in boys—the ceremony of puberty, described in the next chapter.

Among the Incas, children were to remain in the cradle and were almost never removed from it, as the emperor governed even the most intimate details of life. The mother was not allowed to take her child in her arms, so that he not become accustomed to tenderness, and so that "he not learn to demand being carried through weeping or crying." Thus the baby was carried everywhere in his cradle and did not interfere with the daily work routine. To breast feed him the mother squatted beside the cradle and fed him only three times a day, as required by the rules, so that he would not become used to abundance.[95]

Weaning took place at age three.[96] In his *Buen Gobierno*, Felipe Guamán Poma de Ayala relates that the "*uaua quiraupi cac*, breast-feeding infant, . . . must be fed by his mother, and none other but she." The family of an infant of "one, two, three, four, or five months receives no help, aside from that given by the mother, helped by the little brothers or grandmother or aunt or other close relative."[97]

Guamán Poma even describes the type of cradle that was used (Fig. 21). It was made of light wood, with four legs, so that the mother could place it either on the floor on on her back when she left the house. Two arched branches protected the head of the baby, who could thus be wrapped in a shawl without any risk of being asphyxiated. The cradle was held on the mother's back by a shawl crossing her chest.[98]

Romé reports that when the infant was too big to remain confined to the cradle a hole was dug in the ground and cushioned with rags, for the baby to "kick and crawl in."[99] Guamán Poma adds: "[A]t the age of one and two years, the girls are called *llucac uarmi uaua*, which means girls who crawl," wearing an Inca-style hat and a skirt with a wide belt (Fig. 22).[100]

The Incas characterized the different phases of human existence with their usual extreme sense of organization. The first period was that of the "cradle infant," which continued until weaning at the age of two; parents took care of the infant and watched him, "so that he would not be hurt or burned."[101]

Fig. 22. Crawling girl (Guamán Poma de Ayala).

Fig. 23. Boy playing with top (Guamán Poma de Ayala).

Fig. 24. Five- to nine-year-old girl (Guamán Poma de Ayala).

Fig. 25. (a) Twelve-year-old hunter (Guamán Poma de Ayala).

(b) Twelve-year-old hunter (Guamán Poma de Ayala).

The second phase lasted until the age of five; the child was free to play and raise domestic animals. From then until age nine children were slowly educated by the parents' example. They were duly instructed and punished. From the age of nine children could be useful in scaring birds away from the fields. From twelve to thirteen, boys took care of llama herds and set traps for birds with lovely feathers. During that period they also learned the rudiments of craftwork.

The years from eighteen to twenty were marked by abstinence and poverty: "they had no right to love." At age twenty they began to do all the chores by themselves. Only at twenty-five were they considered subjects of the empire, and registered as such in the official records.[102]

Girls began life in much the same way, but were guided toward their future role: they took care of new-born siblings, tended to the fire, and cut flowers. From the age of twelve they were shaved and depilated and received the name of "little shaved ones" (*coro tasque*). They wore a short skirt and went barefoot, perfected their cooking skills and learned to spin, weave, and prepare the alcoholic beverage called *chicha*. They remained chaste until eighteen—upon pain of death.

Women were used as property, things. They constituted a class half way between men and objects; they had fewer rights in their huts than the domestic animals. They rapidly lost their physical attractiveness. They were respected only in their reproductive function (which was given great importance); their activities were far more regimented than those of the men, and they lived lives of unceasing toil and domestic responsibility. If widowed, they were to remain chaste for the rest of their lives.

Girls ran the risk of being selected by the Inca inspectors to be "chosen women" or "virgins of the sun," to be treated as daughters of nobles or given as presents to officials—a most unenviable fate.[103]

There were no schools or formal education program for the children of humble families. Since there was no writing system, there was little to be learned that could not be taught by parents on an everyday basis; and this education by example was the lot of most children.

The sons of aristocrats living in Cuzco received some formal education (see next chapter), as did the "chosen women." Farmers' children helped their parents as soon as they could walk, and thus learned their place in the community.[104]

We must go once again to Felipe Guamán Poma de Ayala's drawings and descriptions to help us understand the life of Inca children until puberty. He presents us (Fig. 23) with a boy of five years, *pucllacoc uamracona* ("playful one"), wearing a fur hat and wolfskin cape, making a circle with a toy top. "These children helped their mothers and fathers as much as they could, and received many beatings and blows to the head if they misbehaved."[105]

We are then shown the drawing (Fig. 24) of "a girl five to nine years of age, *pucllacoc uarmi uamra*, meaning girl who plays: these little maidens

Fig. 26. Bird hunter (Guamán Poma de Ayala).

serve as pages to a *coya* [queen] or a *nustra* [princess], or to older ladies, virgins, or *mamaconas* [priestesses], and help their mothers and fathers to carry firewood or hay. These girls begin to work, spinning delicate silk or whatever they can, bringing *yuyos* [water plants] from the fields, helping to make *chicha*. . . . They are taught cleanliness and, from a young age, know how to spin, carry water, wash, and cook, the work of women and maidens."[106]

He also draws girls called "*pauau pallac* ["who gather flowers"] of nine years . . . who gather *tire queuencha* [dried vegetables], *onquena llachoc* [water plants], *paconca, pinau, siclla* [herbs]. . . . These girls gathered flowers to dye the wool for *cunbis* [fine weaving] of clothes and other things, and gathered the above-mentioned herbs for cooking, drying and storing them for the following year. . . . These girls were nine to twelve years old . . . and also helped their mothers and fathers in all that was required of them."[107]

The same author then describes (Fig. 25a and b) the "*tocllacoc uamracuna* ["boy hunters of twelve years"], who hunt small birds with snares and bird-lime, and others called elegant birds: *quinte* [hummingbird], *uaychau* [brown bird], *chayna* [goldfinch], *urpay* [pigeon]. . . . From their meat they made *charque* [jerky], *petaquillas* ["bundles"].

"And they kept the feathers as such, or for *cunpi* [the fine weaving of feathers]. And for the *uallcanca* [shield]. . . . They had the daily chores . . . of tending the herds and bringing firewood, hay, they spun and twisted [yarns], and helped their elders in other errands."[108]

He also provides us with a drawing (Fig. 26) and description of a boy "at the mature age of twelve years . . . [*mactacona*]," carrying a great net tied with two sticks held in his left hand. Guamán Poma explains that these children were sent to tend and guard the herds; there with snares and birdlime they caught birds called "*uchiva* [goose], *yuto* [partridge], . . . *tacami* [duck], . . . and made *petaquillas* of the meat, keeping the feathers for the *Yngas* [Incas] and *capac apocona* [powerful lords] and for the captains. . . ."[109]

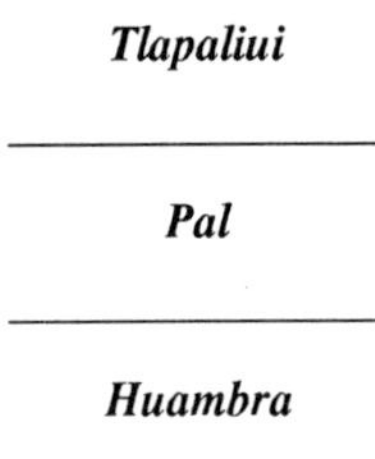

Chapter VIII

YOUTH

At age fifteen or sixteen, and sometimes earlier, as we shall see later on—but always before reaching adulthood—Aztec youths went to two sorts of school, in which they received different types of instruction. One was called the *telpochcalli* (house of youths), for general and martial education, and the other was the *calmécac* (string of houses), for training in priestly duties.

The *telpochcalli* was run by the clan for its members' sons; students were taught citizenship, history and tradition, the obedience of religious norms, and arts and trades—but mainly the use of weapons. The *calmécac* was like a seminary; it provided special training in priestly duties and leadership.

Other schools prepared young girls to be priestesses, and also taught them to weave skillfully and do the featherwork for the priests' garments.[110] The Codex Mendoza[111] (Fig. 27) indicates that young men of sixteen could either enter the *calmécac*, where they were entrusted to the priests, or the *telpochcalli*, generally run by teachers selected from among the clan elders.

The Codex, however, appears to contradict other sources in noting that family education as such ended much earlier. Some parents sent their sons to the *calmécac* as soon as they could walk, and, in any case, says Torquemada, "children began school between the ages of six and nine."[112]

The *telpochcalli* trained youths to be good citizens and warriors. There was a *telpochcalli* for each *cálpulli* or clan attached to the temple. Boys were trained for combat, but also received a strict moral education with instruction in religion, history, customs, chants, dance, and music, with particular emphasis on civic duties.

Fig. 27. Sixteen-year-old boy (Codex Mendoza).

Hard work and severe punishment were accepted norms. Sahagún writes:[113]

> Their life was rough, they all slept in the *telpochcalli*, and they ate in their homes, and he who slept not in the young men's house [the *telpochcalli*], him they punished. And they all went in a group where they did something—perchance they undertook the preparation of mud [for adobes], walls, work the land, make canals. They went in a bunch or they divided into groups. And they went to the forest carrying on their shoulders the wood that was necessary for the *cuicacalli* [the house of song and dance].

Younger boys had to clean the school and temple stairs, tend the sacred fire, carry water, and help the priests to dress; older boys cut firewood and helped those younger than themselves. The priests took fifteen-year-olds to the mountains and made them carry heavy loads of firewood to build their strength, a crucial factor in battle. The boys learned the art of war through constant practice with arms, accompanying armies to the battlefield in order to observe their manoeuvres.

Boys were shaven at the age of ten, but were left with a tuft of hair (*piochtli*) at the nape of the neck, to be shorn off when they captured an enemy. For part of the day students were allowed to visit home and learn a profession from their parents. Conversation with women was forbidden; any boy found alone with a girl was severely punished. Drinking *pulque* was also off bounds; here again transgression was severely punished.[114]

There were three ranks of instructors, according to Peterson: the *tiachcauh* (instructor; literally "older brother"), the *telpochtlato* (head instructor; literally "boss of young people"), and the *tlecatécatl* (school director; literally "settler of men"). The three levels coincided with military ranks, and the right to teach in a school was gained by capturing enemies in battle.[115]

Boys could leave school once they had captured an enemy in battle, or when they married and devoted themselves to farming. The youth who had gone into battle several times without capturing an enemy was held in disgrace; he could leave school but would never be allowed to wear fine clothes or jewelry, or to hold any position of importance in the community. His clothing would be made of cheap material, simply woven. Thus did society insure that military service would be taken very seriously.[116]

The other type of school, the *calmécac*, trained the more promising boys for the priesthood, or for political and military leadership. Only a select few sons of nobles or the most intelligent boys of other social classes were admitted. There was only one *calmécac* per village, with room for about 100 boys; thus few were chosen and discipline was very strict. "Ruler, noblemen, and still others, well mothered, well sired, these same entered their children, promised them, there in the *calmécac*; and still others [did] who wished it," writes Sahagún.

"All became priests—the noblemen because the place of instruction, the *calmécac*, was a place where one was admonished, where one was instructed, a place where one lived chastely, a place where [fleetness of] foot was tested, a place of prudence, a place of wisdom, a place of making good, of making righteous. In no way was there filth, vice. . . ."[117]

All the young ministers of the idols slept in the *calmécac* and swept the temple at sunrise. They could not go home for meals; they prepared their food in the *calmécac* and shared whatever they had brought from home. At midnight they arose to pray and bathe in the fountains.

The older boys were sent to fetch maguey thorns and firewood from the mountains. At eleven o'clock at night they were sent alone up a mountain path with a conch trumpet, an incensor, and some maguey thorns. When they reached a predetermined place they pierced their ears and legs with the thorns, implanting the bloody thorns in balls of grass. They returned while playing their trumpets.

Students were taught to "speak well"; he who did not, or failed to greet appropriately those he met, or remained seated in front of his elders, was punished with maguey thorns. They were also taught the verses of "divine chants," as well as astronomy, dream interpretation, and the calculation of religious and astronomical years.

Religious education prevailed at the *calmécac*, which was built facing the main temple so as to be near the teacher priests. Boys could remain in this learning institution for life, if they so wished, after attaining the rank of *tlanamacac* (priest), though they generally stayed for eight or ten years. The rigorous education and discipline were more like that of a monastery than a school, yet it was a great privilege to enter a *calmécac*, as future judges and political officials were chosen from its ranks.

As we have seen, boys remained near the school for most of the day and rarely saw their parents; they were seldom allowed to go home for meals, as the *calmécac* had adequate supplies of its own. If it did not, the students were sent to beg for food in the streets, but this rarely happened, as each *calmécac* hasd its own farmland and also received part of the tribute sent to the ruler.[118]

It is also doubtful whether there was a class schedule. Classes were probably a mixture of lesson periods, services in the temple, and practical training in the arts and trades. Boys were taught to use the calendar, to interpret and determine the time for religious feasts and rituals to worship the gods, as well as Náhuatl history and civic duty, the functioning of government, and the administration of justice.

Great importance was given to hieroglyphic and pictographic interpretation; boys also learned the medicinal uses of herbs, genealogy, arithmetic, architecture, astronomy, agriculture, and the arts of hunting and war, as well as ritual chants and dances.

It is thought that only six Aztec clans were entitled to send their sons to the *calmécac*. Of these, only members of the Huitznahua and Yopico clans could

become heads of the tribe or high priests of Huitzilopochtli. The *calmécac*
thus tended to divide the tribe into social levels, through predetermined dis-
tinctions. Future aristocrats paid a price for their position: bound to a rigorous
discipline, they received terrible punishment for all transgressions.[119]

Aztec girls also lived within a strict discipline. A chronicler notes that the
Aztecs expected their women to "stop their ears and mouths": they were not
allowed to speak at mealtimes, and had to remain silent for long periods of
time. "They were kept indoors and banned from speaking with boys. They
always went out accompanied by older women who pinched them if they
looked up."

The girls were sent to schools run by priestesses to learn the domestic arts
and religion. Most girls left school to marry, but some stayed and were admitted to special schools in order to become priestesses. Others became midwives or matchmakers. In general, however, women stayed at home and took
little part in social and political life.[120]

Soustelle presents a detailed analysis of the Aztec educational system: Two
options were open to families: the *calmécac* and the *telpochcalli*. The
calmécac was restricted, in principle, to the sons and daughters of dignitaries,
but a passage in Sahagún suggests that the offspring of plebeian families could
also be admitted. This supposition is corroborated by the fact that high priests
were chosen without taking into consideration their "lineage, but rather their
habits, exercises and doctrines and virtuous life"; and priests were necessarily
educated in the *calmécac*.[121]

"On the whole," Soustelle continues, "the 'higher' education given in the
calmécac prepared students either for the priesthood, or for high functions
within the State; and it was extremely severe and demanding. The *telpochcalli*
produced middle-level citizens (which did not prevent some of them from
attaining the highest posts), gave its students much more freedom, and treated
them with much less rigor than the priesthood school."[122]

Education emphasized sacrifice and renunciation, Soustelle notes, quoting
one of Sahagún's sample admonitions to a student:[123]

> Listen, O my son, . . . thou goest not to be honored, to be obeyed, to
> be respected. . . . Thou art only to be sad, to be humble, to live aus-
> terely. . . . Thou art to be diligent in the breaking off of [maguey]
> spines, in the cutting of pine boughs, in the insertion of [maguey] spines
> [in thy flesh], in the bathing in the streams. . . . And when the fasting
> setteth in, when the abstaining from food occurreth, do not break it. . . .
> Do not take it as painful; be diligent in it.

Above all it was a school of self-mastery and inurement. Students learned
to "speak well and express greetings and reverence." "Finally, [the priests]
taught them all the verses of the chants, so that they might sing the so-called
divine chants that were written in their books with characters; and further

taught them Indian astrology, the interpretation of dreams, and the measurement of years."[124]

"Sending a youth to the *calmécac* meant dedicating him to Quetzalcoatl," Soustelle continues; "placing him in the *telpochcalli* meant dedicating him to Tezcatlipoca. Two conceptions of life contended beneath the masks of these divine beings: on the one hand, the priestly ideal of self-renunciation, the study of stars and signs, contemplative knowledge and chastity; on the other, the warrior's ideal which deliberately emphasized action, combat, collective life, the passing pleasures of youth. One of Aztec civilization's most curious traits is that a society so dedicated to war should have chosen the teachings of Quetzalcoatl to train its elite, and should have left those of Tezcatlipoca for the more numerous, but less honored, class.[125]

"Be that as it were, this education fulfilled its mission; it trained its chiefs, priests, warriors, and women. Intellectual instruction as such played a relatively important role only in the *calmécac*, where students were taught all that constituted the national science of the time: reading and writing the pictographic characters, divination, chronology, poetry, and rhetoric.[126]

"It is remarkable that in that time and continent, an indigenous American people should have enforced mandatory education for all, and that no Mexican child of the sixteenth century, whatever his social origin, should have lacked schooling. It will suffice to compare this state of things with that prevailing in Classical Antiquity or the European Middle Ages, to perceive how deeply Mexico's native population, despite its limitations, cared for the education of its youth and the upbringing of its citizens."[127]

Aside from the *telpochcalli* and the *calmécac*, Angel Garibay refers to "specific institutes," such as houses in which natural medicine was taught to the sons of healers, or in which the techniques were imparted for working in feathers, gems, gold, and silver, or the traders' schools, called *pochtecapetlatl*, which taught norms for the complex dispositions governing travel for merchant traders—who also served as spies for the greater expansion of the Tenochca domains.[128]

Bishop Landa has given us a marvelous description of the puberty ceremony among the Mayas. The day was carefully chosen, to insure it would not be an unlucky one. An important man from the community was named the godfather of the participating youths; he was in charge of helping the priest during the ceremony and, even more important, of organizing the party. Aside from him, four honored elders were named *chacs* to help the priest (*chilan*).

On the appointed day they all met at the godfather's house; the ceremony took place in the courtyard, newly swept and strewn with fresh leaves. An elder was chosen to act as the boys' godfather, and an elderly woman as that of the girls. This done, the priest purified the area and a ceremony was held to expel evil spirits. After this rite the courtyard was swept again, more fresh leaves were strewn, and mats were spread upon the ground.

The priest changed his garments, donned a ceremonial coat and a hat like a bishop's miter, made of colorful feathers, and used an aspergillum to sprinkle the holy water that would purify the area. "They set four benches in the four corners of the courtyard, upon which sat the four *chacs* with a thin rope stretched between them, so that the children were as if corraled within the rope; then, stepping over the rope, all the parents whose children had fasted were made to enter the circle. Either before or after this, they set in the middle another bench, upon which the priest sat with a brazier, a little ground corn, and a bit of incense.

Then the boys and girls came to him in succession, and the priest cast upon them a little ground corn and a bit of incense in their hands, and they cast it into the brazier and, having done with the incense, they took the brazier in which it had burned and the rope held by the *chacs*, and poured into a vessel a bit of wine* and gave it to an Indian to be taken out of the village, requiring him not to drink it or look back, and said that thus was the demon expelled.

"The Indian gone, they cleaned the courtyard clear of the leaves taken from a tree called the *cihom*, and spread other leaves from the *copo*, and some mats, while the priest donned his garments. He dressed in a coat of colored feathers, worked with other colored feathers, and other long ones hanging from the ends [of the coat], and a sort of cap of the same feathers on his head, and underneath the coat ribbons of cotton reaching to the ground, like tails, and a sort of brush in his hand, with a short handle, very elaborate, with its hairs made of the tails of snakes which are like rattlesnakes, and all with neither more or less gravity than a pope would have to crown an emperor, and the serenity made by these trappings was great.

"Then the *chacs* went to the children and put on their heads white cloths brought by their mothers. They asked the older ones if they had committed any sin or evil touching, and if they had they confessed to it and were separated from the others.

"Having done this, the priest asked them all to be silent and sit down, and he began to bless the young people with many prayers, and to bless them with his brush, and all with much serenity. After the blessing he sat down and the dignitary chosen by the parents for the feast rose and, with a bone given him by the priest, touched each youth upon the forehead nine times; then he wet him with water from a jar he carried, and rubbed his forehead and face, and in between his fingers and toes, without saying a word. This water was made of certain flowers and cocoa, soaked and diluted in virgin water which, they said, was brought from the hollows of trees or mountain rocks.

"After this rubbing, the priest rose and removed the white cloths from their heads, and others that they wore on their backs, with some feathers from very lovely birds attached to the ends, and some cocoa beans, all of which was gathered by one of the *chacs*, and then the priest cut off from the children,

---

*In Mayan, *balche*: a drink made of the bark or roots of the *Lonchocarpus violaceus*, fermented with honey.

Fig. 28. Eighteen-year-old girl (Guamán Poma de Ayala).

Fig. 29. "Delivery boys" (Guamán Poma de Ayala).

with a stone knife, the bead they wore on their forehead; then the priest's other helpers followed with a bunch of flowers and a smoking object [a pipe] that the Indians used to suck on, and touched each one of them nine times and then gave them the flowers to smell and the smoke to inhale.

"Then they gathered the presents brought by the mothers, and gave each youth a bit to eat, as the gifts were of food, and drank a good glass of wine, and the rest of the gift was offered to the gods with pious prayers, asking them to receive that small gift from the youths and, summoning another official who helped them, whom they called *cayom*, and gave him the wine for him to drink, which he did without resting [taking breath], as it could be called a sin.

"Having done this, the girls first took their leave, their mothers went to remove the band which they had worn about their waist until then, and the shell they wore as a sign of purity, which meant that they could now be married whenever the parents so desired. Then they dismissed the boys and, once they were gone, the parents came to the pile of mantles they had brought and distributed them, with their own hands, to the participants and officials.

Then the feast ended with much eating and drinking. They called this feast Em ku, which means "descent of god." He who had mainly given it and paid for it, after having fasted three days, had to abstain again for nine days and invariably did so."[129]

The girls continued to live with their parents until they married, learning from their mothers how to cook, spin, weave cotton, and perform other domestic duties. Single men painted themselves in black to signify their social status and lived in communal houses where they received instruction in various trades, played games, and openly associated with prostitutes. Referring to these "evil public women," Landa reports that the poor girls devoted to this trade, though paid to do so, were accosted by so many young men that their services were required until the day they died. Marriage was permitted at any time after the puberty ceremony, but did not normally occur until men turned eighteen and women fourteen or fifteen years of age.[130]

Felipe Guamán de Ayala, with his naive drawings accompanied by eloquent texts, once again gives us a glimpse of daily life among Inca youths. He describes (Fig. 28) the *"coro tasqueconas* ["young girls of short hair"] or the *rotusca tasque* ["cropped virgins"] . . . of twelve and eighteen years of age, who served their fathers and mothers and grandmothers, and the principal ladies, to learn to spin and weave delicate things, and tended the herds . . . and made *chicha* for their father and mother, and other activities . . . and cooked for their father and cleaned the house."[131] We may note in the figure how girls tended the llamas, carried firewood, and used the time to spin while they walked.

Further on, the same author describes (Fig. 29) the *"saiapaiac* [messengers], guardians of eighteen and twenty years. . . . [T]hey served as *chacha-*

cona uayna [errand boys] to carry messages from village to village . . . and
tended the herds and accompanied warriors and great dignitaries and lord captains, and took them their food and served the main chiefs of their village.''[132]

Among the Incas the second family feast took place upon the children's
puberty (at thirteen to fifteen years of age), or after the girls' first menses (at
age twelve to fourteen, or sooner). It varied somewhat by region, and was the
equivalent of a second or definitive baptism. It represented the child's entry
into the nation's ranks.

The definitive baptismal name consisted of two parts: a generic part linked
to the *ayllú*, and another personal one linked to the child himself, his merits,
or particular circumstances of his life.[133] The most common names for men
included Robust, Happy, Liberal, Tobacco, Crystal, Falcon, Condor, Jaguar;
and for women, Pure, Star, Gold, Egg, Coca. The offspring of nobles had
several names, some of them honorary or titles of rank.[134]

Ceremonies for men of humble rank were communal; they took place once
a year, and were relatively simple. Boys were given a loincloth that they
would wear from then on, and the main event in the girls' ceremony was to
comb their hair into an elaborate hairdo, as they were no longer the "little
shorn ones.''[135]

The girls' ceremonies took place on an individual or family level. As soon
as the first menses occurred, the girl's relatives were invited to a feast, before
which the girl fasted for three days and could not leave the house. Upon the
third day she could eat a bit of raw corn; the next day her mother bathed and
dressed her with new clothes and white sandals for her to receive and attend
to the gathered relatives. Afterwards, her most important uncle gave her the
name she would bear for the rest of her life, and her relatives proceeded to
present her with gifts.[136]

Curiously, a woman was allowed to leave the *ayllú* and improve her existence if she was beautiful, gracious, or had some special talent; she was
called *nusta* (chosen woman) and was taken to Cuzco or some other principal
city to learn weaving, cooking, and the sun rituals. Such women could marry
high officials or become concubines of the lord Inca himself, as the emperor's
secondary wives prepared his food, made his clothing, and performed his
domestic chores.

Women could also become "virgins of the sun," taking vows of eternal
chastity to become priestesses of the sun. From a tender age they were kept
in "convents" where they were entrusted to the care of *mamaconas* (priestesses) who taught them their religious duties. They also wove for the Inca and
his nobles, and their most important duty was to tend to the sacred fire at
festivals.

The priestesses' links with the outside world were completely severed; only
the Inca or his principal wife could enter their chambers.[137] But, in general
terms, men and women were born, lived, and died in the same *ayllú*, which
gave them complete security in return for their complete adhesion to the rules

of the state.

Puberty ceremonies for the sons of nobles were much more complex and lasted several weeks. They consisted of toilsome demonstrations of manhood, held annually for those noble boys who had reached puberty the previous year. These rites were meant to test the youths' physical and psychological abilities, and to determine what posts they could fill, as the Incas believed that higher rank implied greater demands. Thus noble youths were not treated with benevolence; on the contrary, they were judged more harshly and were expected to surpass all others in physical strength and in their capacity to endure punishment.[138]

Like other mountain tribes, the Incas celebrated the rites of puberty so their youths could receive the responsibilities and prerogatives of the warrior. The ceremony is worth describing not only because of its intrinsic interest, but also because it came to be the principal ceremony of the State; it was through this ritual that the aristocracy received the insignia of its superiority.

The ceremony was called *capac raymi* (great festival), and took place in the month equivalent to December. The month's climax and principal ritual was called the *huarachicoy* ("the celebration of the shorts or loincloths"). Closely related to it within the same complex ritual was the rite of the *tocochicoy* (perforation of the ears), which culminated in the placement of enormous earrings—at which moment the boys became true *incas pakayoc* (men with earrings) or "big ears," as the Spaniards called them.[139]

Aside from marking their entry into adult life, the ceremonies tested young boys' resistance to suffering, the awakening in them of the warrior spirit, and their tribal learning. They began with a period of fasting and sexual abstinence, during which time women wove the special garments to be worn for the ceremonies. Girls were especially assigned the weaving of loincloths highly ornamented with fringes.

The youths were bound to a very tough routine of great physical activity on a very poor diet, during which they had to climb the slopes of Cuzco to gather hay, with which they would decorate the sandals and make the chairs for the tribesmen at the ceremony.

The ceremony officially began when the candidates for induction met in the square, on the fifth day, to be presented to the emperor and the *huacas*, the mummified ancestors. Before the youths stood the pantheon and all the tribe's history—the world they would enter if they were found worthy.

After this they were taken to the foot of Huanacauri (the sacred mountain). The white llama had a place of honor in the procession, as it was the symbol of Inca prosperity. The youths were accompanied by their own *mamaconas*, who carried jars of *chicha* on their backs for them to drink and *coca* for them to chew.

On that and two more nights the boys slept in the cold of the mountain slopes, imploring the *huacas* to give them the courage and help they would need in the next few days. On the tenth day they presented themselves before the *huaca* of the Huanacauri, and the priests gave them the leather or cotton slings which were the characteristic weapon of the Incas. The priests and elders who served as mentors to the boys beat them with the slings, so that their bodies might feel directly the moral virtues of these warrior instruments. (See also Chapter IX.)

Back in Cuzco, the boys carried out a ritual dance in the square, during which spectators flogged them on their arms and legs. Aside from the tension, these tests obviously included pain and hunger, and had to be accepted by the boys with composure and humility. He who lost his spirit or showed pain disgraced his family and the *huacas*.

On the fourteenth day, the boys dressed in special garments and, accompanied by nubile girls from the tribe carrying jars of *chicha*, climbed the mountain again to carry out various rituals. The girls went down to pre-established spots near the foot of the mountain, from where they spurred the boys on with cries and promises of *chicha*.

Then took place the most difficult of all the tasks: a race down the mountain, at top speed, in which the youths could lose their lives or become permanently crippled (which often happened). The first boy to reach the bottom and drink the *chicha* proffered by the girls was honored with great pomp. This part of the ceremony reflected the masculine tradition of drinking *chicha* served by the women of the tribe; some authors believe the ceremony actually ended with a sexual orgy.[140] Three other mountains had to be climbed before the rites ended—the Sahuaraura, the Yahuira, and the Analmaque.

On the twenty-first day the boys purified themselves at the fountain of Callispuquio. On Yahuira mountain they were arrayed in splendid warrior costumes, had their ears pierced to receive earrings later on, and received their definitive names, just as the girls had received theirs at the end of the menstrual rites.

Thus they went up the mountain as boys and came down as adult men, members of the noble caste of Inca warriors. The next day in the square each one was invested with the arms of war, given by an uncle. Other relatives presented rich gifts, while giving them a strong blow and the recommendation that they be loyal and brave. The emperor himself gave them the earrings, made of silver and gold.

During the final ceremony the young men engaged in a savage warrior dance, dressed in puma or jaguar skins and feathered headgear, exhibiting their fierceness in battles to come. This was followed by a four-day feast, attended only by the most noble Incas, who danced, sang, and drank *chicha* of course.

As regards the education of young people, the famous statement by Tupac Inca Yupanqui cited by Garcilaso de la Vega, "El Inca," points to an enormous cultural difference between Mesoamerican and South American civilizations:

Fig. 30. Quipu (Guamán Poma de Ayala).

It is not right that the sons of plebeians should be taught sciences which belong only to the generous, that such low people might raise themselves and puff themselves up and criticize and belittle the republic; it is enough for them to learn their fathers' trades, for leading and governing are not for plebeians, and it would be an offense to the office and the republic to entrust such tasks to the common people.[141]

The Inca monarchy looked after its subjects, satisfied their physical needs, established moral laws, and gave them attention and affection as a father does his children; but it always considered them children, with no right to act or think for themselves, whose only duty was to understand their bond of blind obedience.

Thus, higher learning was only for noble youths who, after the puberty ceremonies (at around age fifteen), entered seminaries to receive instruction in four areas: the Quechua language, religion, the *quipu*, and the history of the kingdom. These seminaries were entrusted to the *amautas* (wise men), who served as teachers to the young nobles.

It is known that some Inca princes built their palaces near these schools, that they also attended classes taught by the *amautas*, and sometimes offered their own homilies. These royal students were instructed in the different fields of their teachers' competence, with special reference to the position they would occupy in life. They studied the laws and administrative principles of the government they would eventually enter. They were initiated into the peculiar rites of their religion, very necessary for those who would one day assume priestly functions.

They also learned to emulate the feats of their ancestors by listening to the chronicles of the *amautas*. They learned to speak their own dialect with purity and elegance, and studied the mysteries of the *quipu*, which allowed Incas to communicate ideas among themselves and transmit them to future generations.[142]

The *quipu* was a length of twine about two feet long, made of twisted strings from which hung other, shorter strings, as in a fringe. The strings were of different colors and came together in knots (the word *quipu* means knot). The colors represented different objects: for instance, white signified silver and yellow, gold. The colors could also signify abstract ideas: white could mean peace, and red, war (Fig. 30). But the *quipu* was mainly used for arithmetical purposes: the knots represented digits which could be combined to signify numbers in any amount, serving as a mnemotechnical device.

Each district had its *quipucamayas* (guardians of the *quipus*), who used the *quipu* to compile data on royal sales, volumes of raw or processed materials in the district, as well as to register births and deaths. This information, preserved on the multi-colored *quipu* strings, constituted the equivalent of a "national archive," in Prescott's words.[142]

The *quipu* was thus excellent for arithmetical calculation, but it was poor at representing ideas or images. It served, however, as a memory aid (by association of ideas) to the *amautas*, helping them to remember and teach the history of the empire. The narration of events was transmitted by oral tradition, and the *quipus* helped chroniclers to organize facts with methods and sequences.

Once history was stored in the mind and remembered in detail, thanks to frequent repetition, it was transmitted by the *amauta* to his pupils; thus was oral tradition passed on to successive generations, aided by the *quipu's* arbitrary signs. There were probably many discrepancies in the details, but the general idea was preserved. The Inca *quipu* was far beneath the Aztecs' pictographic writing or the Mayas' hieroglyphics, which, as we are now beginning to learn, were able to represent some quite sophisticated thinking.

Chapter IX

GAMES AND TOYS

A book devoted to children would be incomplete without a chapter on their games and toys.

The literature, however, on precolumbian life is very poor, and it is regrettable that when Sahagún and the translator of the Codex Mendoza compiled their wealth of data on everyday living they did not ask their informants about this engaging topic—as they did, for instance, regarding the more uncomfortable matter of punishment.

This omission is perhaps understandable if we consider that the compilers of these works came from a Western culture which gave little importance to children as human beings, as discussed earlier.

Child's play is a little-understood phenomenon, as is proven by the many theories that have attempted to explain it. Among writers who have studied it are various important psychologists, such as Jean Piaget, Schneerson, and Karl and Charlotte Buhler.[143] There are psychosocial theories of play, such as Shiller's theory of "excess energy," the "recreative theory" of Lazarus, Hall's "recapitulation theory," and Mitchell's "self-expression" theory—none of which is really applicable to precolumbian cultures.[144]

Perhaps Spencer's "theory of preparation for the future" would be the most applicable in this regard.[145] It asserts that

> . . . a child's play tends to have the form of adult activities. . . . Man does not play because he is young, but because nature makes him go through a period of childhood so that he can play, and thus prepare himself for adult activities.

81

Fig. 31. Toltec toy(?)

Fig. 32. Inca doll.

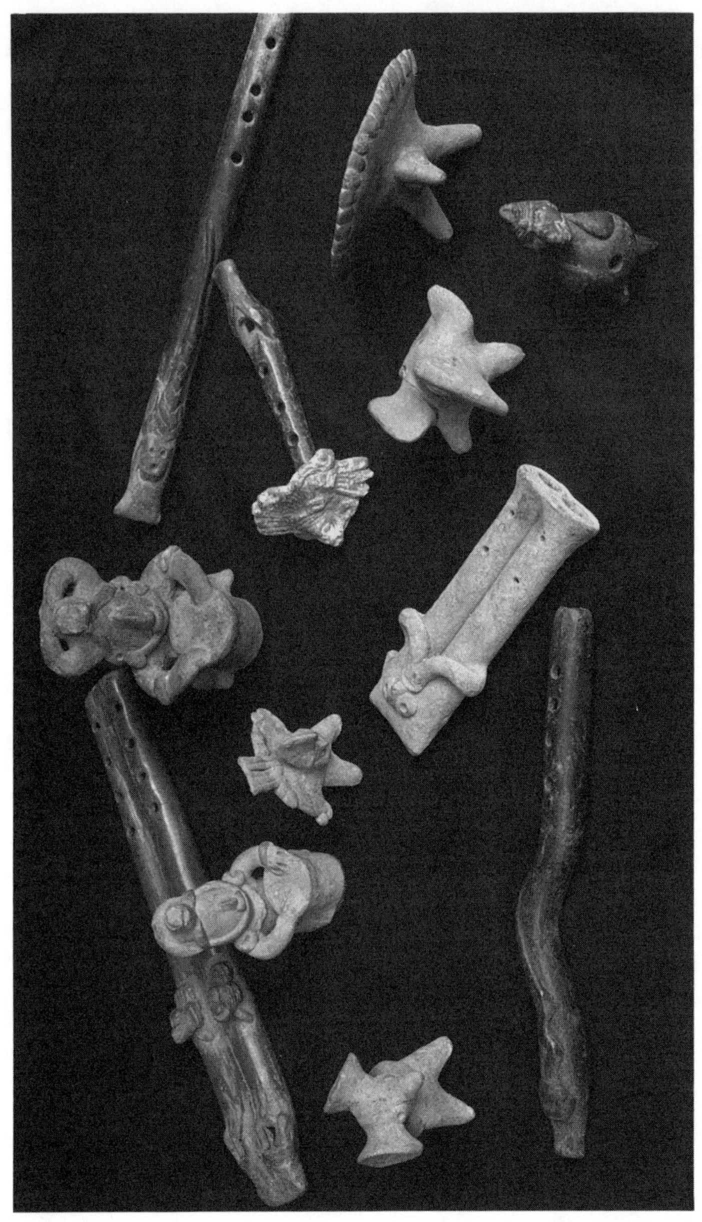

Fig. 33. Flutes and whistles, Aztec and western Mexican cultures (from the author's collection).

This is precisely what happens in all primitive cultures: children perform activities—helping in the preparation of food and other household chores—that parallel those of adults. What has been described in previous chapters is obviously encompassed by this theory, though only partially.

The psychosocial theories are complemented by psychoanalytic theories of play which cannot adequately be described in a book of this scope. I will limit myself to Erikson's practical scheme,[146] which views play and the phases of child development and establishes three types of play according to the child's age:

(A) Autocosmic (autospheric) play: The child's play is centered on his own body, and consists in exploring his own kinesthetic and sensory perceptions and vocalization.

(B) Microcosmic (microspheric) play: This is the small world of graspable objects; if that first use of things is successfully handled and correctly guided, the pleasure of mastering objects becomes associated with mastery of the traumas projected therein. This is a difficult period for children, as they must confront a world that has its own laws, in which adults can remove toys at will, or toys can become broken, causing a great deal of anguish.

(C) Macrocosmic (macrospheric) play: Finally, as the child reaches school age (an actuality for Aztec children) play enters the macrosphere —the world shared with others. The child learns that the content of play is accepted only in fantasy, as in microcosmic play.

Perhaps now, drawing upon the theories of Spencer and Erikson, we may view the play of precolumbian children, within the rigid limits imposed by adults, as preparation for the future—as a process of "learning to learn," within the family circle and later, within the school environment.

There is little documentary evidence concerning the existence of toys. But various authors accept as toys the Toltecs' little terracotta animals with wheels (Fig. 31)—though other scholars see them as funerary offerings[147]—raising the question of wheels for children but not for adults! Other such toys would be the Toltec terracotta dolls with articulated arms, and those dressed in lovely clothing typical of Inca textile manufacture.

There are also tops (Fig. 23) and—why not?—the nets to hunt butterflies and birds (Fig. 26) recorded by Guamán Poma de Ayala.[149] We know that Aztec children played with tops, as there is a word for them in Náhuatl, *pepetotl*.[150] There is evidence that Inca children also played with them (Quechua *piscoynu*).[151]

We also find the doll (Fig. 32) among the Mayas (*al'che*), as it also appears among the Aztecs (*nenetl*) and the Incas (*huahua pucllana*). The kite flown on

Fig. 34. Tlachtli—precolumbian ball game
(Florentine Codex).

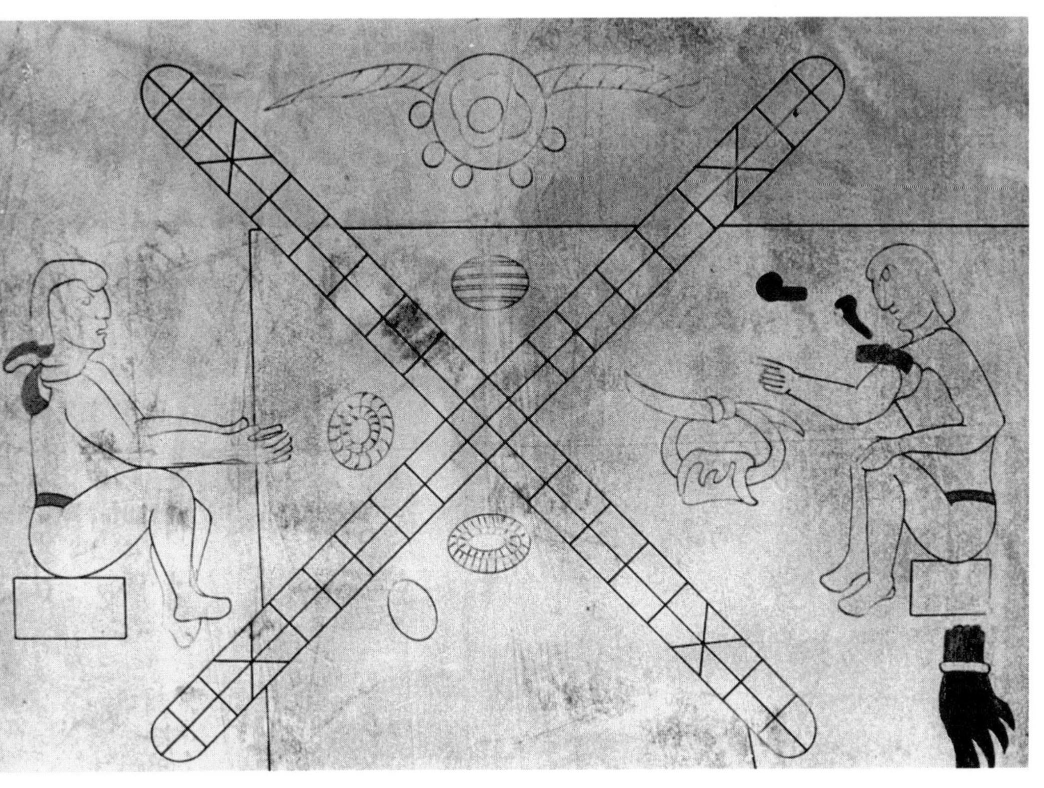

Fig. 35. Patolli—precolumbian board game
(Florentine Codex).

a string derives its name in Spanish (*papalote*) from the Náhuatl *papalotl* (butterfly);[153] it is *chuuklan* (comet) in Mayan.[154] And what can be said of all the musical instruments—whistles, flutes, and percussion instruments—that we know were used (by adults) at feasts and religious ceremonies (Fig. 33); who knows what wonderful sounds they produced, and what pleasure they must have given the children into whose hands they fell!

One of the few passages about children's play is provided by Landa;[155] I repeat here the account from Chapter VII: ". . . but throughout their childhood they were pretty and playful, always going about with their bows and arrows and playing among themselves." It was natural that all their fathers' hunting and combat activities would especially become the subjects of their games, no doubt reenacted with careful attention to detail and, as observed by their parents, approved with deadly seriousness.

Many of the Aztecs' formal games have come down to us:

Tlachtli (the rubber ballgame; *poctapoc* or *pocolpoc* among the Mayas—Fig. 34)[156] and *patolli* (a game like parchesi—Fig. 35)[157] were adult games, soaked in religion and mysticism; ball courts and *patolli* playing boards (scratched onto benches) appear throughout Mesoamerica. It might be appropriate to infer there were versions for children, though there is no documentary evidence for this. This being so, and as there are many excellent accounts derived from Sahagún, Durán,[158] and, more recently, Piña Chan,[159] I will not delve into them more deeply.

We do know of other games with less mystical-religious content, which makes it more likely they were imitated by children: Bernal Díaz del Castillo relates how, during the captivity of Moctezuma, "with Cortés he played *totoloque*, a game they call thus."[160] This game consisted of tossing small pellets made of highly polished, smelted gold onto some quoits, also made of gold, which served as targets. Five hits were sufficient to win. Obviously, such a simple game could well have been played by children with stones or seeds.

Various Aztec ceremonies ended with races (*paynatotoca*), in which runners competed for the favor of the gods. "They trained from childhood in the exercise of racing," Piña Chan explains.[161] The Mayan term for races is *alkab*.[162]

Mesoamerica also knew the game of jumping over other children, now called leapfrog. In Mayan it is *tip kusam*.[163] Piña Chan also describes the game of little holes (*cocoyoc-patolli*) and *chichinadas* (marbles).[164] Durán notes that[165]

> . . . many of the Indians' games were of much subtlety and skill and art. . . . Who does not see the subtlety and great skill in carrying a thick stick, one and a half *brazas* long [about 60 inches], with such nimble feet . . . performing so many turns and leaps, throwing it to the sides and up high, catching it with the soles of their feet, with an ease I greatly admire. . . .

The same sources also describe the game in which two young men spin, with hands interlaced, building up their speed until one of them falls.

Among the Incas, as well as the Aztecs, many games or pastimes had mystical or penitential meaning, as in the lashings given with ropes or straps. This was done with some frequency, for instance, during the puberty rites described in Chapter VIII. But it was also practiced as a game, to test each other's resistance to pain—though this was probably prohibited before adolescence.

Guamán Poma de Ayala refers to children playing (*pucllacoc uamracona*) in the text for Fig. 24. Among the Inca games we know of, I shall describe those which, by virtue of their simplicity, were probably also played by children. There was the *wayru*, a sort of "snakes and ladders" game (like *patolli*); the *chuncara*, played with different-colored grains or seeds which were tossed onto a polished stone perforated with holes of different values. The game of *apaytalla* consisted of using one's fingers to expel a seed from its pod, making it jump as far as possible; the sound it made was also a factor in the competition.[167]

Races and other common athletic games were reserved to members of the noble class; the "big-eared" youths could participate in them only from adolescence on.[168]

Chapter X

CHILDHOOD DISEASES AND THEIR THERAPY

As we have seen, birth, puberty, marriage, and procreation were the high-lights of family, religious, and social life among precolumbian cultures. This explains the prominent role played by "obstetrics" and "pediatrics," which were actually a combination of magic and empirical knowledge.

When we described birth rites in Chapter V we noted the uncertainty regarding the ills awaiting a newborn child, expressed in the following prayer: "we know not if you will live long among us."[169] Coury interprets this as an allusion to the high infant mortality of that time, and cites the skeletal remains found in Sonoma, California. Fourteen percent of them belonged to newborn infants and 25 percent to children and adolescents from one to nineteen years of age. And 48 percent of the human remains found in Mesa Verde, Colorado (going back to 750-1300 A.D.) are those of children and adolescents less than twenty years old.[170]

Healers enjoyed great prestige in precolumbian societies. Thanks to Sahagún once again[171] we know of the Aztecs that they took very seriously the healer's profession and moral duties. Religious and magical medicine was taught in temples called *tepoxtlato*, and empirical medical knowledge was usually passed on from father to son; teachers were called *tlamatini*, and pupils, *momachti*.[172]

Coury also believes that fever convulsions were not uncommon in children and were related to the *ciuapipiltin* (specter women, souls of those who died in childbirth). Also common was a depression (*tocuacoyoyan*) of the fontanelles (the boneless areas of a baby's skull), which did not escape Aztec observers.[173]

Among the Mayas, priests received instruction in the divinatory arts, the principles of arithmetic, and the use of medicinal plants. Those who devoted themselves to medicine were admitted to the "profession" in a religious ceremony called *pocan*, which took place in the month of Uo, and in which they received the small idols, magical objects, and herbs which they would use in their daily practice.[174]

Among the Incas, "doctors" belonged to the privileged class of the *amautas* and were called *callahuyas*; they were usually recruited from the valleys near Lake Titicaca and made up a sort of priestly brotherhood devoted to medical-religious activities.[175] Their professional practice was subject to certain rules, described in detail by Garcilaso de la Vega.[176] They also had herbalists, *hampi camayac*, who knew how to find and prepare many medicinal herbs.[177]

Child pathology had no particular characteristics, though most of the infectious and contagious diseases of viral origin were unknown before the Conquest. One finds in Sahagún some direct mention of childhood diseases and their treatment. If we add to these the general illnesses that are frequent in children to this day, we might compile a small treatise on Aztec pediatrics —especially if we were to include in it the references to childhood illnesses translated directly from the Florentine Codex by López Austin, which appear in his book, *Textos de Medicina Náhuatl.*

Sahagún relates:

[For infected ear:] Its cure is to apply drops of tepid *coyoxochitl* sap [*Polanisia uniglandulosa*] with chili in the ear thrice daily; also the same by night. These bring out either phlegm or pus. And the scrapings of seashells with salt in tepid [water] are applied in drops in the ear. . . .

[For ear ulcers:] Pulverized *coyoxochitl* [leaves] mixed with a pine resin are applied on the outside as a poultice, and, mixed with *axi* [an oil made of crushed insects], pressed in the openings [of the ulcers]. And they are continually washed with urine. And [the herb] *cicimatic* [a root plant, *Conavallia villosa*] with [the white of] an egg is applied; [or] all the medicines for infections—*chichi[patli], chipili* [a medicinal herb, *Astragalus mollis*], avocado pits.''[178]

[For] Snuffles, which affects little babies. Morning dew is dropped into their nostrils, and [drops of] woman's milk, and *cimatl* sap [an edible and fermentable root, *Desmodium amplifolium*]. And the inside of their mouths is massaged with tomato juice or with salt.*[179]

The stopped nostrils [of children]. The nose is anointed with salve of pine resin. . . . And one is not to drink cold things; only tepid [or] hot

---

*The morning dew is perhaps a better remedy than the water drops prescribed by modern-day pediatricians!

things is one to drink [and] eat. And one is to take care not to come upon—not to encounter—the cold. Also one is not to expose himself to the sun.*[180]

[For hoarseness:] Many times the throat is massaged with liquid rubber [*Hevea brassilensis*]. And bee honey is to be drunk, and many times, through the nose, bee honey or thickened maguey syrup will drop [into the throat].[181]

[For mumps, or swelling of the throat:] Its cure is massage—vomiting. And [the herb] named *cocoxiuitl* [a medicinal plant, "turtledove herb," *Bocconia arborea*], with lampblack, is placed on the throat. And water of the *ahacaxilotic* [a medicinal, "cane herb," is drunk].[182]

[For coughing:] As its cure, there is to be vomiting, there is to be massaging of the throat. One is to drink [an infusion of] *tlacopopotl* root [unidentified], [or] lime water mixed with chili, [or] the water of cooked wormwood; [or] one is to drink [an infusion of] the root [of an herb] named *pipitzauac* [a medicinal plant, *Petresia adnata*]. . . . He will avoid the cold, the chill; he will cover himself well. Also the sweat bath will help him."†[183]

According to López Austin diarrhea was cured with *coyotómatl* ["coyote tomato," *Vitex mollis*]; diarrhea with blood with the root named *tzipipatli* [unidentified].[184] He also cites various psychological problems; for instance, children stuttered because "though grown, they continue to suckle." It was thus believed that children should be weaned early, "that they be given food promptly."[185]

Sahagún devotes several paragraphs to the problems of agalactia (inability to furnish milk) and infections of the nipple in nursing mothers:

She is to drink [an infusion of] *tzayanalquiltic* root [unidentified], which is to be pulverized with a stone. Then one is to wash her breasts with saltpeter. Or [she is to drink the infusion] many times when she comes from the sweat bath. But when the first milk flow comes, when it comes anew, it will still give the child diarrhea.[186]

[For breast tumor:] Herbs named *ixyayaual* ["frame of the face," unidentified] and *eloquiltic* [an edible corn plant and medicinal] are cut, [ground up, and] mixed together. These bring it [the tumor] to a head or dissolve it. And if they bring it to a head, it is to be lanced.[187]

*One can almost hear a grandmother's voice in this instruction!
†Perhaps the Spanish influence changed this latter recommendation to a ban on bathing, an idea still popular in modern times.

Appendix III of Sahagún's history in Garibay's edition describes the child healer, who "when a child is sick in the chest, sucks him with wormwood. Either she sucks blood, or pus, so that some heal and others do not."[188]

At the end of Appendix III we are told how a depression of the fontanelles was treated: "the healer . . . holds the child head down and shakes his head from side to side. She presses on his palate; . . . some use their breath and also press the palate and stuff it with cotton; some [children] heal with this, others do not. . . ."*[189]

Among the Mayas, Guerra[190] gives us some idea of the illnesses which affect children, especially diarrhea, with a great variety of descriptions suggesting it was very common among them. "Dysentery, *hubnak puuch*; choleriform syndrome (a gastrointestinal disturbance), *pu tac*; dysentery with tenesmus (violent desire to defecate), recalling amoeba syndrome, *tur*." The common cold was called *izkah*.

The Mayas grouped the most frequent contagious diseases among children under the name *hamyaah*; itchiness was called *zahil*, scabies, *ueez*. Among throat pathologies, they distinguished pharyngitis, *yacalil*.

It is difficult to compile a catalog of Inca childhood diseases like that provided by Sahagún for the Aztecs. As Guerra explains in the exhaustive *Historia Universal de la Medicina* of Laín Entralgo,[191] the Incas "identified diseases only by their particular symptomatology: hemorrhages, *usputay*; abscesses, *chupu*; pus, *qqiesa*; vomiting, *quepney*; diarrhea, *quechay*; coughing, *uhui*; fever, *rupha*; pain, *nanay*.

"There are some descriptions of illnesses which make them recognizable, such as *coto*, endemic goiter (which undoubtedly appeared in childhood), due to a lack of iodine in their diet, common in the Cuzco area."

Garcilaso de la Vega notes that "breast-feeding infants . . . especially if they had fever, were washed with urine in the morning, . . . and when they could collect the baby's own urine, gave him some to drink. When children were born, they cut the umbilical cord at about a finger's length. . . .[T]hey preserved it with great care and gave it to the child to suck upon any indisposition. . . . [I]t had to be his own, for they said that another child's was of no use."[192]

The Incas also perforated the nasal bone, and progressively flattened the head with boards called *tsuko*.[193]

---

*Various Náhuatl enchantments and spells for toothache and earache are described in the short and exquisite book by Laurette Sejourné cited in the Bibliography.

Chapter XI

CHILD SACRIFICE

As we have seen time and again, precolumbian peoples everywhere gave great love and attention to their children. So it might seem incomprehensible that we should also find eloquent references—leaving no room for doubt—to the ritual sacrifice of children practiced, to a greater or lesser degree, by all the peoples of ancient America.

Once again, it was Friar Bernardino de Sahagún who first realized that such practices were a part of Aztec religion and culture, and not the product of parents' natural cruelty. He explains this himself in what he calls the "Author's Exclamation":[194]

> I do not believe there can be such a hard heart that can hear of such inhuman cruelty [as child sacrifice]. . . . Such cruel blindness, executed upon those unhappy children, must not be blamed upon the cruelty of the parents, who spilled many tears, but rather upon our ancient enemy, Satan. . . .

Sahagún relates that, in the first month of the year (called Atlacahualco and corresponding to February), in honor of the rain god Tlaloc:

> In this month they slew many children; they sacrificed them in many places upon the mountain tops, tearing from them their hearts, in honor of the gods of water, so that these might give them water or rain. The children whom they slew they decked in rich finery to take them to be killed; and they carried them in litters upon their shoulders. And the litter went adorned with feathers and flowers.

[The priests] proceeded, playing [musical instruments], singing, and dancing before them. When they took the children to be slain, if they wept and shed many tears, those who carried them rejoiced, for they took [it] as an omen that they would have much rain that year. . . .[195]

In another chapter he tells us that

. . . they assembled the children whom they slew in the first month, buying them from their mothers. And they went on killing them in all the feasts that followed, until the rains really began. And thus they slew some in the first month, named Atlacahualco; and some in the second, named Tlacaxipeualiztli; and some in the third, named Toçoztontli; and others in the fourth, named Uei toçoztli.[196]

In a later chapter Sahagún gives us a detailed description of the Aztec child-sacrifice feasts celebrated in the first month of the year:

. . . they took children, known as "human banners"—those who had two cowlicks of hair and whose day signs were favorable. They were sought everywhere, and bought. It was said: "These are precious blood-offerings. [The rain gods] receive them with rejoicing; they wish for them; they are thus satisfied and given contentment." With them, the rains were sought; rain was requested. . . .

And all went with headbands with sprays and sprigs of quetzal feathers; they had green stone necklaces, and they went provided with green stone bracelets; they provided them with bracelets of green stone. Their faces were painted with liquid rubber, and spotted with a paste of amaranth seeds.

And their liquid rubber sandals: they had sandals of liquid rubber. All went in glorious array; they were adorned and ornamented; all had valuable things on them. They gave them paper wings; wings of paper they had. They were carried in litters covered with quetzal feathers, and in these [the children] were kept. And they went sounding flutes for them.

All mourned much; men wept for them; men loosed their tears for them; they mourned them and they groaned. And when they reached the place of vigil, in the Mist House, here was spent the night in vigil. . . .

And if the children went crying, their tears coursing down and bathing their faces, it was said and understood that indeed it would rain.[197]

Children were sacrificed in seven different places: Quauchtépetl (near Tlaltelolco), Yoaltécatl (near Guadalupe), Tepetzinco (on a lagoon near Tlaltelolco), Poiauhtla (near Tlaxcala), Pantitlán (which was an eddy in the lagoon of México), Cócotl (near Chalco), and on Mount Yauhqueme (near Atlacihuaya).

Carlos María Bustamante's edition of Sahagún (1829) states at this point: "They killed many children in these places each year, and afterward cooked and ate them."[198]

Sahagún describes other ceremonies which took place every four years in the eighteenth month (Yzcalli). There was a ceremony in which "very early in the morning, before dawn, they began to pierce the ears of the boys and girls, and they applied to their heads a wig of parrot feathers, pasted on with *ocotzotl*, which is pine resin."[199]

This ceremony, also described in another chapter, took place during the *nemontemi* or barren days, on the last days of the year (in our calendar, the four last days of January and the first of February):

> There is conjecture that when they pierced the boys' and girls' ears, which was every four years, they set aside *six* days of *nemontemi*, and it is the same as the [leap year] which we observe every four years.

Entering into greater detail, he continues:

> Early in the morning was begun the boring of ears, when they pierced the ears of the small children. And they pasted them with yellow parrot feathers and with soft, white feathers, which went mixed with the yellow ones. . . .
>
> And the mothers sought out some master of the youths, seasoned warrior, or leader of young men, who might wish to be a parent, thus to become their [children's] uncle. Also, some sought out a woman who might be an aunt, and they offered her gifts. . . . And for this reason [the feast] was named Izcalli [the growing]: at this time they lifted by the neck all the small children. It was said that thus they grasped them for growth, that they might quickly mature.

This was the only occasion upon which children were permitted to get drunk, during a feast called Pillahuano, which means "the children all drink wine," and all gave wine to drink to the small children.[200]

Friar Bartolomé de las Casas also describes the child sacrifices in honor of Tlaloc, god of water:

> . . . they sacrificed a boy and a girl of three or four years, children of nobles and principals, not slaves, . . . and took them in a canoe . . . and in the middle of the lagoon, or Lake Mexico, threw them in the water.[201]

This ceremony, which he also describes in another chapter, took place during the *nemontemi* or barren days, the five last days of the year which were considered unpropitious, unlucky.

The same author relates (from reports he received) how

> . . . every three years they killed three children and took out their hearts and the blood thereof, and with a gum called *ulli* [rubber] that comes from a tree grown in hot lands, which, when it is pricked produces white drops which later turn black, from which they make the balls with which they play, which bounce six times more than ours. . . .
>
> [W]ith this liquor [the rubber] and the blood from the children's hearts and certain seeds ([from] the first [produce] to come out of an orchard around their temples) they prepared a mixture and a dough which [my informant] asserts was used for communions and other superstitions.[202]

It is interesting that las Casas refers to what he interprets as circumcision rites,[203] which are now seen as simple scarifications or punctures inflicted on the foreskin of the penis, done to gather a few drops of blood. They could also be gathered from the earlobes or other extremities, and were used in religious rites usually involving adults, not children.

Morley states that Maya women and children were sacrificed as frequently as men.[204] And Bishop Landa asserts that, in order to carry out these sacrifices they would purchase the children of slaves, or else those of people who "out of devotion delivered [up] their children, who were greatly regaled until the day of the feast."[205]

Virginity was an important requisite for sacrifice; thus the large number of children who were requisitioned as "pure victims," which Landa explains as a reference to "their absence of carnal sin." If necessary, the victims were bought or kidnapped from neighboring towns.[206]

In the first exploration of the sacred well of Chichén Itzá, Edward H. Thompson found 21 skeletons of children between the ages of eighteen months and twelve years, as well as 13 adult men and 8 adult women.[207] In 1967 another exploration of the well was undertaken, and hundreds of human skeletons were found, most of which belonged to children.[208]

In the tomb of Palenque, in a crypt in front of that of the personage of Eight Ahau, six skeletons were found of young people between the ages of sixteen and eighteen years. As the discoverer of the tomb explains, "this was a human sacrifice of youths whose spirits were meant to guard and serve the person for whom the entire, enormous pyramid had been built."[209]

Though it is evident that South American cultures practiced sacrifice less frequently than the Aztecs and Mayas, there are very early accounts by Bandera, Polo, and Piderahita, cited by Guerra, which give detailed descriptions of sacrifices among the Chibchas.[210]

There are also references to child sacrifice in the earliest literature. Girolamo Benzoni, for instance, states that "they sacrificed men and children" in the provinces of Quito and Peru; López Gómara relates that "the Incas often sacrificed their own children."[211]

José de Acosta provides one of the most vivid and lengthy descriptions:

> . . . they were accustomed in Peru to sacrifice children of four to six years—up to age ten, and this mostly in matters affecting the *Inga* [the reigning conqueror], as when he was sick, to bring him health, or when he went to war, to bring him victory. . . .
>
> And when they gave the tassel, which was the king's insignia, as here the scepter or crown, to the new *Inga*, during the solemn feasts they sacrificed a quantity of two hundred children aged four to ten years; a hard and inhuman spectacle. They had various rituals and ceremonies to sacrifice and bury them; at other times they cut their throats and rubbed themselves from ear to ear with their blood.[212]

Acosta asserts that although "the Mexicans exceeded those of Peru in the number of men they sacrificed, and the horrible way in which they did so, . . . yet those of Peru exceeded the Mexicans in killing and sacrificing their children, as I have not read or heard that this was done among the Mexicans."[213] Acosta apparently had not perused the codices!

Burr Brundage tells us that the Incas held two special ceremonies, outside the monthly calendar of feasts: the *capacoha* and the *itu*.[214] The *capacoha* was a petition presented by the entire population upon the emperor's coronation, at the outset of a military campaign, or upon the emperor's illness; the gifts made to the gods were "their most prized possessions, their children, . . . whose hearts were taken out and offered to Viracocha."

The *itu* ceremony took place upon the occasion of disasters, plagues, or earthquakes, as well as during the monthly ceremonies described by Acosta and other authors, such as Cieza de León[215] and Mason.[216] We are told that at least one important ritual took place each month, related to the relevant agricultural ceremony. At these feasts llama sacrifices played an important role; upon rare occasions children were sacrificed and their blood offered to the gods.

**Fig. 36. Ixtlilton the healer god of Aztec children
(Codex Borbonicus).**

Chapter XII

IXTLILTON

THE HEALER GOD OF AZTEC CHILDREN

Here is a description of Ixtlilton of the Aztec children, a cultural phenomenon unique in history: a deity exclusively for children, illustrating the love and devotion of precolumbian peoples for their children.

Sahagún describes Ixtlilton's appearance (Fig. 36):

. . . he was spread over with unguent; his face was covered with soot; about his lips white clay was placed. He had a crest of flint knives with quetzal feathers added. The burden on his back was a fan of red arara feathers. His sun flag stood upon it. His paper shoulder-sash had sun emblems. Sun emblems were on his shield. Red was his staff, upon which was a heart. He had a necklace of rock crystal. He had a paper breech-clout. He had bells, he had shells. He wore sun sandals.[217]

We may see representations of him in the Codices Borbonicus[218] and Borgia.[219]

The god with the black or blackened face (his name comes from the roots *ixtli*, face, countenance, and *tlilli*, the color black) was the god of medicine, according to Siméon,[200] invoked to cure sick children. This "blackface," also called Tlaltetecuin, is considered one of several invocations of Tezcatlipoca.

Sahagún continues:

This god had a temple made of painted wood, like a tabernacle, which contained his image. In this tabernacle or temple there were many bowls and tubs of water, all covered with planks of wood or sheets of metal. They called this water *tlilalt*, which means black water, and when a child sickened they took him to the temple or tabernacle of this god Ixtlilton, and uncovered one of the tubs. They gave the child to drink of the water, and he became whole.

When one wanted to worship this god with a special feast, his image was taken to the home. This was not sculpted or painted, but was a dignitary dressed in the ornaments of the god, and incense was burned before him as they carried him, until this image arrived at the home where the feast was to be held, with dances and chants, as they used to do, because their manner of dancing is very different from ours.

I describe here the manner of these dances, also called *areytos*. . . . [T]hey joined by twos or threes in a great chorus, according to their number, bearing flowers in their hands and ornaments with feathers; they all move together, with hands and feet, a wondrous and skillful thing to see. All their movements followed the beat of the drummers playing the drum and the *teponaztli*.* . . .[221]

With these sounds of dancing, drums, and the *teponaztli*, dedicated to the recovery of sick children, we must now leave the magical world of the precolumbian child.

*A kind of drum used by the Indians in the *areytos,* or religious dances, to accompany their chants. The instrument consisted of a hollowed tree trunk, with two long slits in the upper part, played with two sticks with rubber balls on the ends. The resulting sounds made a sort of scale with a minor third.

Chapter XIII

EPILOGUE:

THE HISTORY OF CHILDREN

''The history of children is a nightmare from which we have only recently begun to awaken'' is the epigraph at the beginning of this book.[222]

It was only at the end of the last century that Wilhelm Preyer, a German physician interested in his own child's development, kept a diary entitled *Die Seele des Kindes* (The Mind of the Child),[223] an essay that awakened interest in the study of children. Toward the end of his life the same author supervised the editing of Louise Hogan's book, *A Study of a Child*.[224]

Sigmund Freud based his psychoanalytical theory on child sexuality[225]—yet it is curious that he made no reference to the history of children, though he had a profound knowledge of world history in general which provided him with the bases or illustrations for many of his hypotheses.

At the close of the last century pediatrics became established as one of the four basic branches of medicine, together with internal medicine, surgery, and obstetrics. At that time many historical aspects of children's diseases were discovered—but the history of childhood has yet to be written!

The works cited in the first chapter of this book are very incomplete and limited in their scope. George Payne's work is made up of a series of unrelated essays on various primitive cultures. The work of French historian Philippe Ariès is only a social history of childhood at the time of Louis XIII, drawing upon that king's personal history. Abt-Garrison's history of pediatrics places more emphasis on the history of childhood diseases, but with little attention given to the social and human condition of children.[228]

Lloyd De Mause's work is a series of fifteen essays covering various historical periods,[229] and stems from the intensive research done by a group of "psycho-historians" who appeared on the psychoanalytical scene in the United States in 1974. David Hunt's work[230] describes the psychology of family life in seventeenth-century France.

The conclusion of all this literature on childhood is negative, as I have mentioned in the first chapter. The concept of love and respect for children barely dates from our own century.

Having reviewed the history of precolumbian children in these pages, we emerge with a much more positive vision—and this despite the well entrenched *ritual* practices of sacrifice and bodily deformation!

As Miguel León-Portilla has already noted in his *La Filosofía Náhuatl*,[231] and restated in his later book entitled *Toltecayotl: Aspectos de la Cultura Náhuatl*, "There is certainly a great deal of first-hand information about the *tlacahuapahualiztli* (the art of raising and educating men)."[232] There are basically two phases in the education of Aztec children that León-Portilla brilliantly and concisely summarizes:

(1) The education given at home . . . by the father . . . with a kind heart . . . which is support with protecting hands. . . . [H]e raises and educates [his] children, teaches, and admonishes them. . . .

(2) The second phase is the process of *tlacahuapahualiztli* [which] began with the child's entry into the educational establishments which we would today qualify as public [institutions].

There is a profound abyss separating Mesoamerican cultures (it is not so great in the case of South America) from European and Asian cultures in this regard. It undermines the economic explanations insistently given by historians for the latter cultures' contempt for children.

There is proof of the Mesoamerican natives' intense love for their children, which I hope has been evidenced by this text. As León-Portilla states in the aforementioned works, the goal of Aztec education was "profoundly humanistic." As proof, he quotes a text by Sahagún—actually a lovely poem dedicated to little girls—who, in other cultures, were even more discriminated against than boys:

> The little girl, little creature,
> turtledove, little one,
> tender one, well fed . . .
> Like a jade, a bracelet,
> divine turquoise,
> quetzal feather,
> precious thing,
> the smallest one

> *worthy of care,*
> tender child who cries,
> creature clean and pure.[233]

The Incas' "humanism" toward children is not comparable to that of the Aztecs, since the rigidity and interference of the State in all aspects of life was absolute. Yet we also find in their culture lovely poems wishing a long life for children:

FIRST PRAYER TO THE NEWBORN
Cause of being, Viracocha,
God always present,
Judge of all that is,
God who provides and foresees,
Who creates with merely saying:
"Be a man, be a woman,"
Give freedom and peace
To the being you made
And raised.

Where are you? Outside,
Or in, within the cloud
Or in the shadow?
Hear me, answer me,
Let me live for many days,
Until the age must come
For white hair.

Then raise me,
Take me up in your arms
And if I tire, help me
Wherever you are, Father Viracocha.[234]

Appendix A

SUPERSTITIONS IN THE AZTEC HOME

Aside from the superstitions described throughout the work of Friar Bernardino de Sahagún, he also devotes his Fifth Book to "the omens in which the Mexicans believed," and its Appendix to "the different things which God's creatures, the idolators, wrongly believed."

From the latter I quote several passages referring to children and not included in the text of this book. The reader may recognize some of them as possible sources for our "modern" popular advice on raising children, whether Mexican or international.

Here are Told the Different Things that
God's Creatures, the Idolators, Wrongly Believed[235]

The Fifth Chapter, which telleth of stepping over one

As to stepping over one, the natives [were] also deluded. When some child lay stretched out across one's path, if someone stepped over him then they chided him who passed over him, saying to him, "Why dost thou step over him?"

It was said that thereby the child would grow no more; he would only be small. And in order to cure him, so that [this] might not befall the child, once again he stepped back over him. Thus it was remedied.

The Sixth Chapter, which telleth of drinking

As to drinking [any liquid], there also was a delusion of the ancients, somewhat like the account of stepping over one.

And in this wise was the account of it: when, perchance, one drank; if one yet a small child drank first, and afterwards one drank who was a little older, already grown, then [the elder] restrained and took the water from the small child. He said to him: "Why dost thou wish to drink first? Thou wilt not grow large, but remain small. Now let thy older brother drink, for he is already bigger."

The Seventh Chapter, which telleth of him who dipped into the cooking pot

Of this there was also a delusion of the natives, known especially of the men. And in this wise was it known: when, perhaps, men were eating, and one only dipped into the cooking pot—not into a sauce dish—then also the mothers and fathers restrained him. They said to him: "Do not dip into the cooking pot; there [in combat] thou wilt leave thy captives. If thou goest to war, none wilt thou seize; no one will become thy captive."

The Eighth Chapter, which telleth of tamales stuck [to the cooking pot]

Concerning *tamales* stuck [to the cooking pot] as another deception of the natives, it was said that the men and women would not eat them. It was stated that if the men were to eat them, when they would shoot arrows in warfare the arrow which was shot would not find its mark. Or perchance therefore they might die, or one's wife would bear children with difficulty.

And just so was it as to a woman. If she were to eat *tamales* which had stuck [to the pot], she could not bear children. Her child would only adhere to and thus die in her womb. Therefore the mothers sternly forbade them to eat *tamales* which had stuck [to the cooking pot].

The Eleventh Chapter, which telleth of the woman lately delivered

Another thing the natives did in their folly. When they would visit one who had [just] borne a child, if they took their [own] children with them, they then quickly placed ashes on their temples, knees, and shins, and everywhere [did they place ashes]. And the woman who applied the ashes sat before the hearth. It was said that, if they did not place ashes on the knees of the children, when they walked, their knees, wrists, ankles, would creak.

The Twelfth Chapter, which telleth of earthquakes

When the earth quivered, a delusion of the natives was to be seen. When the earth quaked, then they quickly took their children by the neck and lifted them, so that they might soon grow big—so that they might mature quickly. It was said that if they did not take them by the neck and lift them quickly, they would wax larger with difficulty. And they said that the earthquake would bear [the child] away if they did not grasp him by the neck and lift him.

The Thirteenth Chapter, which telleth of the [three] hearth stones

Concerning the [three] hearth stones, there was also a delusion of the natives. When they saw someone kicking the hearth stones, they restrained him from doing so. They said to him: "Do not kick the hearth stones. It will deaden thy feet when, perchance, thou goest to war." They said to him that now he would not be able to walk or run in time of battle. His feet would be numbed; quickly he would fall into the hands of their foes. Hence the natives restrained their youths, that this might not befall them.

The Fifteenth Chapter, which telleth of small children who licked the surface of the grinding stone

When small children licked the surface of the grinding stone, the mothers chided and scolded their young ones for it, and restrained them from it, saying to them: "Do not lick the grinding stone; your teeth will thus quickly break and fall out." Because of this, they filled their children with great fear, so that this would not befall them.

The Sixteenth Chapter, which telleth of him who leaned against a post

When they saw one who leaned against a post, there also was folly of the natives; they chided him for it, and restrained him from doing so; they prevented their children from doing it. They said to them: "Do not lean against the post; it is a liar." Thus did they speak: "It giveth one lies; it is like unto one who lieth." [With] this, they terrified the children lest such might befall them and they tell lies.

The Seventeenth Chapter, which telleth of the maidens who ate standing

In times past, when the natives saw their maidens eat standing, they also restrained them from it. They prevented their children from doing so. They said to them: "Eat not while thou art standing. Thou wilt marry far from here. Who will follow thee?" It was said that it would befall one that she would marry in a distant place; she would be taken somewhere far away, not in her own *pueblo*, where she lived.

AZTEC FATHERS' ADVICE TO THEIR SONS

The Twenty-second Chapter[236]

Here are told the admonitions of the father, nobleman, or ruler, to counsel his son regarding prudence in public, and how to sleep, to drink, to eat, to talk, and how to dress. And he told him never to eat anything from the hands of the whores, the harlots, because they feed one, they cause one to drink bad food, their [unsafe] potions.

Behold still a word to finish my talk. Perhaps I shall deceive [you] if I have hidden a word left by our forefathers as they departed, in order that thou mayest dwell with others on earth, in order that thou mayest be prudent in all things, in everything.

First: thou art to be one who riseth from sleep, one who holdeth vigil through the night. Thou art not to give thyself excessively to sleep, lest it will be said of thee, lest thou wilt be named a heavy sleeper, one who goeth falling asleep, a constant sleeper, a dreamer.

By night thou art to arise, thou art to pass the night awake, thou art to sigh, to cry out, to make demands of our lord, the lord of the near, of the nigh, the night, the wind. And thou art to turn quickly to the sweeping, thou art to take care as thou art to hold vigil, as thou art to arise, in the offering of incense.

And second: thou art to be prudent in thy travels; peacefully, quietly, tranquilly, deliberately art thou to go, to take to the road, to travel. Do not throw thy feet much, nor raise thy feet high, nor go jumping, lest it be said of thee, lest thou be named a fool, shameless.

Neither art thou to travel very slowly, nor to drag thy feet, lest it be said of thee that thou art a dragger, thou art a lout, thou art a fat one; lest it be said of thee that thou goest waddling, that thou goest like a mouse; also lest thou turn thyself into an object of derision, incline thy head, travel like a pregnant woman. Nor art thou to go trampling; thou art not to seem like a firefly, not to strut, not to bustle about, lest it be said of thee that thou art only an old thing, that thou art shameless.

Also thou art not to hang thy head, not to incline thy head much, not to stand up off balance, not to look sideways, not to look out of the corner of the eyes, lest it be said of thee that thou art an imbecile, very much a commoner, that thou hast not been counseled that thou art very much an orphan, that thou bringest thy orphanhood upon thyself.

Third: thou art to speak very slowly, very deliberately; thou art not to speak hurriedly, not to pant, nor to squeak, lest it be said of thee that thou art a groaner, a growler, a squeaker. Also thou art not to cry out, lest thou be known as an imbecile, a shameless one, a rustic—very much a rustic. Moderately, middlingly art thou to carry, to emit, thy spirit, thy words. And thou art to improve, to soften thy words, thy voice.

Fourth: thou art to pretend not to dwell upon what is done, what is performed. Especially art thou to depart from, to forsake, evil. And thou art not to peer at one, not to peer into one's face, not to stare at one. Thou art not to peer into the face, at the head of—not to stare at—the esteemed one, especially a woman; much less at someone's wife, for it is said he who stareth at, who peereth into the face of another's wife, with his eyes commiteth adultery, and that some were imprisoned, punished, or put to death, for this.

Fifth: Guard, take care of thy ears, of that with which thou hearest. Do not gossip; let what is said remain as said. Ignore it. Pretend not to understand the words. If thou canst not ignore it, respond not. And speak not; only listen; let what is said remain as said.

And when something is said, if something evil is told there, what meriteth death, and on thee—if thou dost withdraw with others, if thou actest foolishly with others, especially if thou lendest a word, if thou speakest among others —on thee it will be laid; [then] thou wilt expiate the words of others, thou wilt atone for others, and thou wilt be taken, thou wilt be seized, and furthermore, thou wilt be imprisoned.

It is said, because of thee words will be denied, there will be defending, there will be excusing. And he whose words they are, perhaps he is there, perhaps he remaineth thereby virtuous, and perhaps he is content. But thereabouts thou art made a fool.

Thus this is very necessary; thou art to be prudent, O my precious son. Do not die somewhere in vice, do not die somewhere in vain. Take good heed, take care; see to it that thine eyes are open.

Sixth: when thou art summoned, be not summoned twice, be not called twice. The very first time, thou art to arise responding, to arise quickly. If thou art to be sent as a messenger, thou art to run, to be swift. If thou art ordered to get something, thou art to get it promptly. Thou art to travel swiftly, to travel bounding, in no wise sluggish, like the wind art thou to go.

Thou art to be diligent, and thou art to do things at only one bidding, for if thou art twice summoned thou wilt be considered as perverse, lazy, languid, negligent, or thou wilt be regarded as one disdainful of orders, as a haughty one. This is the time when the club, the stone, should be broken on thee.

Seventh: as thou art to array thyself, as thou art to clothe thyself, thou art not to dress vainly, thou art not to array thyself fantastically, thou art not to place on thyself the gaudy cape, the gaudy clothing, what is embroidered. Neither art thou to put on rags, tatters, an old loosely woven cape.

The unhappy, the discontented, our lord honoreth with this, giveth as merit, giveth as one's lot, so that he causeth them to be the miserable, the useless, the unhappy, the discontented ones, to suffer tribulation, pain. The forest, the plains, they completely cover; they go searching for the herbs, the wood, the wild bean, the roots. Thou art not to imitate this, not to take joy in it, not to find merit in it; for it is a matter of ridicule. This is what it meaneth.

Thus art thou to tie on thy cape: do not tie it on so that thou goest tripping over it; neither art thou to shorten thy cape. Moderately art thou to tie it on. Nor art thou to expose thy shoulder. The *quachicque*—the so-called furious [men] in war—they who goeth confidently encountering their death, and the entertainer, and perhaps the buffoon, or perhaps the dancer and the mad one, all snatch the cape of whatever kind; they drag it, they trip over it, they go about mocking, they go rudely, they go drawing it to the armpit, shoulder bared; they go in conceit, graceless, dragging their feet, twisting and turning as they travel.

And their sandals [*cactli*, or footwear in general] are wide and long, the straps dragging, and their excessively long sandal thongs [also] dragging. But as for thee, be thou always prudent as to the cape and the sandals; place on thee what is always good, proper, all fine.

Eight: Listen! Above all thou art to be prudent in drink, in food, for many things pertain to it. Thou art not to eat excessively of the required food. And when thou doest something, when thou perspirest, when thou workest, it is necessary that thou art to break thy fast. Furthermore, the courtesy, the prudence [thou shouldst show] are in this wise: when thou art to eat, thou art not to be hasty, not to be impetuous; thou art not to take excessively nor to break up thy *tortillas*. Thou art not to put a large amount in thy mouth; thou art not to swallow it unchewed. Thou art not to gulp like a dog, when thou art to eat food.

Thou art not to let thyself choke on the food, not to strangle. Thou art to drink, to eat slowly, calmy, quietly. Thou art not to stir up the pieces, not to dig into the sauce bowl, the basket. Take care lest the choking on food, the strangling, should befall thee there.

How hath it come about that thou hadst caused laughter at the place of eating? Quickly hadst thou fallen to the ground if thou hadst choked. And they would mock thee for it; a great quantity of what is savory they would arrange for thee, for thou wouldst yet nourish thyself. But because thou wert a glutton, thou wouldst fall to the ground when thou wert to eat. Rather, thou wouldst be intemperate. Therefore also art thou a spectacle.

And when already thou art to eat, thou art to wash thy hands, to wash thy face, to wash thy mouth. And if somewhere thou art to eat with others, do not quickly seat thyself at the eating place with others. Quickly thou wilt seize the wash water, the wash bowl; thou wilt wash another's hands.

And when the eating is over, thou art quickly to seize the wash bowl, the wash water; thou art to wash another's mouth, another's hands. And thou art to pick up [fallen scraps], thou art to sweep the place where there has been eating. And thou, when thou hast eaten, once again art thou to wash thy hands, to wash thy mouth, to cleanse thy teeth.

In brief, these are as many words as I give thee, as I now cause thee to hear; as many words lie guarded, those to live by, those worthy of being guarded. Our forefathers, the old men, the old women, the white-haired ones, the white-headed ones, departed leaving them. The many words—O that thou couldst later take them to heart!

Right here are a word or two which merit being taken, being guarded, being grasped, which our forefathers went [to heaven] putting in their coffers, in their reed chests; for all courtesy, all prudence, comes from [and] are taken from this.

They went saying that on earth we travel, we live along a mountain peak. Over here there is an abyss, over there is an abyss. Wherever thou art to deviate, wherever thou art to go astray, there wilt thou fall, there wilt thou plunge into the deep. That is to say, it is necessary that thou always act with discretion in what is done, what is said, what is seen, what is heard, what is thought, etc.

And further, behold, thou art to take care, thou art to go remembering, not to swallow things carelessly; thou art to leave a little. What thou wilt see, or whatever is placed before thee, thou art not to eat quickly, for on earth there are inhuman conditions. There are inhuman people, evil ones, haters of men, who will somewhere cause thee to swallow something in drink, in food. Proceed cautiously with thine enemies, or those who were thine enemies. Especially art thou to proceed cautiously with, to live in fear of, the women —above all, the whores. Thou art not to eat, thou art not to drink the things offered [by them]. Such is said of the evil ones, the disloyal, the agitators, those with potions. Some, it is said, seek revenge.

This, it is said, is pleasurable: one [potion] causeth one to discharge one's fluid when the whores, the harlots, cause one to eat it, swallow it, or drink it, to provoke lewdness. This endangereth one; and it is very deadly because one is dried up. For it useth up our blood, our color, our oils; it useth up our moisture, it useth up the turpentine, the resin [of our bodies].

So, it is said, he who partaketh of *maçacoatl** is moderate [who] drinketh it moderately. [If immoderate] he will have carnal access to perhaps four, five, perhaps ten women. And to these women he hath access not only once with each one, but four or five times with each one, more or less. And no one endureth. He who partaketh of the *maçacoatl*, if aggressive, quickly dieth. As he dieth he becometh well dried up, veritably [only] a little lock of hair, having long tufts of hair, locks of hair, on the face.

Perhaps he had been a mere child; perhaps he endureth for some time; perhaps he liveth yet a while; perhaps he continueth in the service of our lord. Eventually he is only little old eyes, only little locks of hair, tufts of hair, very white, nasal mucus hanging, trembling of neck; the flesh only hangeth in wrinkles; he quickly dieth.

Guard thyself well, O my son. Perhaps someone giveth thee something to be eaten, to be drunk. If thou art suspicious of him, let him eat first, let him drink first what he giveth thee. Pay attention. Continue with caution on earth, for thou hast heard that moderation is necessary.

*Literally "deer serpent"; "a kind of worm with horns," "a big, inoffensive serpent"; apparently an aphrodisiac.

AZTEC FATHERS' ADVICE TO THEIR DAUGHTERS

The Eighteenth Chapter[237]

Here it is related how the rulers admonished their daughters when they had already reached the age of discretion. Thus they urged them to prudence [and] virtue, public [and] private. They placed before them, revealed to them, the nobility, the government, the honor, that they should in no way blacken, dirty, discredit, the lineage. Very good were the words with which they admonished them.

Here art thou, thou who art my child, thou who art my precious necklace, thou who art my precious feather, thou who art my creation, my offspring, my blood, my color, my image. Now grasp, hear, that thou hast come to life, thou wert born; that our lord of the near, of the nigh, the maker, the creator, hath sent thee to earth.

And now that thou hast become knowledgeable, already thou observest how things are. There is no rejoicing, there is no contentment; there is torment, there is pain, there is fatigue, there is want; torment, pain, dominate. Difficult is the world, a place where one is caused to weep, a place where one is caused pain. Affliction is known. And the cold wind passeth, glideth by. Most certainly on one the wind lesseneth the heat. And it is a place of thirst, it is a place of hunger. This is the way things are.

Hear well, O my daughter, O my child, the earth is not a good place. It is not a place of joy, it is not a place of contentment. It is merely said it is a place of joy with fatigue, of joy with pain on earth; so the old men went [to heaven]

117

saying. In order that we may not go weeping forever, may not die of sorrow, it is our merit that our lord gave us laughter, sleep, and our sustenance, our strength, our force, and also carnal knowledge in order that there be peopling [of the earth].

All make life gay on earth in order that no one go weeping. And although it is so, although this is the way of life on earth, is it perhaps therefore heard, is it perhaps therefore feared, is life perhaps therefore lived in weeping? For there is living on earth; there is one's becoming an eagle warrior; there is one's becoming an ocelot warrior.

And who is saying that this is how it is on earth? Who is just yielding to death? For there is the doing of things; there is the providing of a livelihood; there is the building of houses; there is labor; there is the seeking of women; there is marriage; there is the marriage of women to men; there is the marriage of men to women.

And now, O my daughter, hear it well, look at it deliberately; for behold, here is thy mother, thy noble one. From her womb, from her breast, thou wert chipped, thou wert flaked. It is as if thou wert an herb, a plant, which hath propagated, sprouted, blossomed. It is also as if thou hadst been asleep and hadst awakened.

See, hear, and know how it is on earth. May thou live, may thou just live, may thou continue a little. In what manner wilt thou live? In what manner wilt thou continue a little? They say the earth is a dangerous place, a fearsomely dangerous place, O my daughter, O dove, O little one.

Know that thou comest from someone, thou art descended from someone; that thou wert born by someone's grace; that thou art the spine, the thorn, of our lords who went [to heaven] leaving us, the lords, the rulers, who already have gone to reside beyond, those who came guarding the realm, and who came giving fame, who came giving renown to nobility.

Hear this: Especially do I declare unto thee that thou art a noblewoman. If thou wert only to esteem thyself as a precious person! This, even though thou art a woman. Thou art a precious *chalchiuitl* [green stone], thou art a precious turquoise. Thou wert cast, thou wert perforated [i.e. conceived among blood sacrifices?]. Thou art blood, thou art color, thou art a spine, thou art a thorn. Thou art one's hair, one's fingernail, one's chip, one's flake.

And so now I say to thee: dost thou perchance not yet take much heed? Dost thou perchance pile up earth, [and] potsherds [i.e. play]? Art thou perchance on the surface of the ground [as a child]? For already thou hearest a little, thou beholdest a little.

Do not, just of thy own accord, bring dishonor upon thyself. Do not in something cause embarrassment to our lords, the lords, the rulers, who have gone leaving us. Do not be a commoner; do not lower thyself.

Thus art thou to conduct thyself on earth among others, for verily thou art a little woman. Here is thy task which thou art to do: be devout night and day. Sigh many times unto the night, [unto] the wind [as a god]. Plead with, speak to, cry out to him, stretch out thine arms to him, especially at thy reclining place, at thy sleeping place.

Do not practice the pleasure of sleep; awake and arise promptly, awake with a start, at the parting of the night; support thyself on thy elbows, thy knees; arise promptly, make thy bow, incline thy head. Speak to, cry out, to the master, our lord, to him of the night, the wind, for he rejoiceth to hear thee by night, and then he will show compassion to thee, he will give thee what is thy desert [task], thy merit.

And thy desert, thy merit, which thou wert given in the beginning, with which thou wert arrayed, into which thou camest to life, into which thou wert born: if it was not good, at this time it will be made good, it will be made favorable. The master, our lord, the lord of the near, the nigh, will change it.

And at night hold vigil, arise promptly, extend thy arms promptly, quickly leave [thy bed] soft, wash thy face, wash thy hands, wash thy mouth. Seize the broom: be diligent with the sweeping; be not tepid, be not lukewarm. Wash the mouths [of the gods; i.e. idols in the home]; especially do not neglect the offering of incense, for thus is our lord petitioned; it is the means by which his mercy is requested.

And when it is so, when thou hast made preparations, what wilt thou do? What wilt thou seize upon as thy womanly labors? Is it perhaps the drink [making *chicha*?], the grinding stone? Is it perhaps the spindle whorl, the weaving stick? Look well to the drink, to the food: how it is prepared, how it is made, how it is improved; the art of good drink, the art of good food, which is called one's birthright. This is the property of—it belongeth to—the lords, the rulers.

Thus it is called, it is named, one's birthright, the food of rulers, the drink of rulers, the food of noblemen, the choice drink, the choice food. Look with diligence, open well thine eyes, apply thyself well to how it is done, for thus thou wilt live and thus thou wilt acquire things, and thus thou wilt be loved, even if it is doubtful, undetermined, where our lord assigneth thee.

If perhaps already the misery of the nobility dominateth, look well, apply thyself well to the really womanly task, the spindle whorl, the weaving stick. Open thine eyes well as to how to be an artisan, how to be a feather worker; the manner of making designs by embroidering; how to judge colors; how to apply colors [to please] thy sisters, thy ladies, our honored ones, the noblewomen. Look with diligence; apply thyself well [in weaving] as to how heddles are provided, how ties are provided, how the [design] template is placed. Take care not to fail to know, not to lose through neglect, not to lose through carelessness.

Now is the opportune time, and it is yet a good time. Thy heart is yet a precious green stone, yet a precious turquoise. It is still keen; nothing defileth it; it is still untouched, nowhere twisted, still virgin, pure, undefiled.

And we [parents] are still here, we who have had great regard for thee. Wilt thou perchance say, thou who art our child, "I make myself, I form myself"? It was our affair; we have suffered for thee; but thus the world endureth. Was it perhaps so ordained? For our lord declared, determined, the propagation, the multiplication [of man] on earth.

We are still here; it is still our time. The club, the rock, of our lord fall not yet. And not yet do we die, not yet do we perish. Take heed, O my youngest, O dove, O little one!

When our lord hath hidden us [i.e. when we die], thou wilt live by the grace of others. The herbs, the woods, the strands of chili, the cakes of salt, the enriched soil are not thy desert, not thy gift, [nor] art thou to frequent another's entrance, because thou art a noblewoman. Pay good attention to the spindle whorl, the weaving stick, the drink, the food.

Perhaps there will happen what is not conceivable, what is not expressible. Someone will select thee, will speak for thee [in marriage]. If [thou art] unable in anything, how will it be? It will not for this reason be thrown in our faces. And if our lord hath hidden us, there will be no murmuring against us therefor in our absence; we will not be chided therefor in the land of the dead. And thou wilt not move, thou wilt not separate condemnation from thyself.

But if already thou payest attention to the same, wherefrom cometh the reprehension? To [such] a purpose thou wilt glorify thyself by one's grace, thou wilt esteem thyself, thou wilt be proud. It is as if thou wert to be of the order of eagles, of the order of ocelots. Well art thou to assume thy shield; may possibly all the little shields [children?] rest in thy hand.

Also there, because of thee we will raise up our heads; thou wilt render us honor. But if thou dost nothing well, perhaps it will not be said of thee that thou art without lice [i.e. thou may indeed be censured]. Seldom wilt thou bathe. And which of the two ways will our lord wish for thee?

Especially note what I say to thee, what I cry out to thee. Thou art my creation, thou art my child. Take special care that thou not dishonor our lords from whom thou art descended. Cast not dust, filth, upon their memory. May thou not dishonor the nobility with something.

May thou not covet carnal things. May thou not wish for experience, as it is said, in the excrement, in the refuse. And if truly thou art to change thyself, wilt thou become as a goddess? May thou not have quickly destroyed thyself. Yet calmly, with special care, present thyself well.

If it so please our lord, if someone so will demand, will speak for thee [in marriage], thou art not to reject, to kick away, the spirit of our lord. Take him. Thou art not to refuse; thou art not to retreat twice, not to retreat thrice; thou art not to resist.

Although we are the parents, and although thou art born of goodly parents, thou art not to overesteem it; thou wilt offend our lord. For that he will pelt thee with dust, refuse, debauchery; [and] this same one will delude [thee], will be capricious.

Do not trade, do not deal, as if in the market place. And do not, as in the summertime, go looking for the best. Do not languish from desire. Howsoever he [the prospective groom] may be—perhaps truly upstanding or perhaps only [average] in any manner—do not reject the one sent by our lord. If thou dost not consent thou wilt be ridiculed, for truly he deludeth [thee], he will turn thee into a harlot.

But meanwhile present thyself well, look well to thine enemy that no one will mock thee. Give thyself not to the wanderer, to the restless one, who is given to pleasure, to the evil youth. Nor are two, [or] three, to know thy face. . . .
When thou hast seen the one who, together with thee, will endure to the end, do not abandon him. Seize him, hang on to him, even though he be a poor person, even though he be a poor eagle warrior, a poor ocelot warrior, even though he be a poor warrior, or a poor son, or one who struggleth for existence. Do not detest him therefor. Our lord, the wise one, the maker, the creator, will dispose for you, will array for you.

This is all I give thee of my word to comply with my duty unto thee, before our lord. Perhaps somewhere thou wilt reject it. Thow knowest it. Meanwhile, I do my duty. O my daughter, O my child, O dove, O little one, pay close heed. May our lord keep thee in peace!

REFERENCES

Chapter I. Prologue: Children in History

1. Karsh, p. 8.
2. Abt-Garrison, Ch. 1, p. 2.
3. De Mause, Ch. 1, p. 1.
4. Abt-Garrison, Ch. 1, p. 7.
5. Ibid., p. 10.
6. De Mause, Ch. 1, p. 27.
7. Payne, Ch. III.
8. Abt-Garrison, Ch. 1, p. 3.
9. Ibid., p. 10.
10. Ariès, p. 39.
11. Karsh, p. 16; *Oxford Dictionary of Quotations*.
12. Abt-Garrison, Ch. 1, p. 4.
13. Ibid., pp. 6, 29.

Chapter II. The Precolumbian World

14. Dubos, Ch. 1, p. 15.
15. Piña Chan (1960), Ch. IV, p. 37.
16. Engel, Chs. I, II; von Hagen (1957), Chs. I, II; Mason, Ch. II.
17. Soustelle (1955), Chs. I, II; Guerra (1971), Ch. II; Bernal (1976), p. 125.
18. Morley, Chs. I, II, IX, X, XI, XII.
19. Romé, Chs. 1, 2, 3; Guerra (1971), Ch. II.

Chapter III. Pregnancy

20. Sahagún (1978), Bk. VI, Ch. 14, pp. 135-36.
21. Ibid., Ch. 15, p. 143.
22. Ibid., Ch. 25, pp. 146-47.
23. Ibid., Ch. 26, p. 149.
24. Ibid., Ch. 27, p. 151.
25. Ibid., Ch. 27, p. 152.
26. Martínez Cortés, Ch. II, p. 145.
27. Soustelle (1980), Ch. V, p. 189.
28. Sahagún (1975), Appendix 1, p. 898.
29. Sahagún (1978), Bk. VI, Ch. 27, pp. 155-56.
30. Ibid., pp. 156-57.
31. Sahagún (1829), Vol. II, Ch. 27, p. 181.
32. Soustelle (1980), Ch. V, p. 190.
33. Whitlock, Ch. 5, p. 72.
34. Ibid.
35. Ibid.
36. Mason, Ch. 9, p. 146.

Chapter IV. Childbirth

37. Sahagún (1978), Bk. VI, Ch. 28, p. 159.
38. Ibid.
39. Cruz, p. 128.
40. Coury, Ch. XI, p. 182, quoting the 1945-48 work of Derbez and Sordo Noriega.
41. Sahagún (1978), p. 160.
42. Sahagún (1978), p. 161.
43. Soustelle (1980), Ch. V, p. 191.
44. Coury, p. 183.

45. Ibid., p. 185.
46. Landa, Ch. XXXII, p. 58.
47. Guerra (1972), Vol. I, p. 309.
48. Mason, Ch. 9, p. 147.

Chapter V. Birth

49. Sahagún (1978), Bk. VI, Ch. 30, p. 167.
50. Ibid., p. 168.
51. Ibid., pp. 171-73.
52. Soustelle (1980), Ch. V, p. 169.
53. Clavijero, Bk. VI, Ch. 38, p. 193.

Chapter VI. Baptism

54. Vaillant (1950), Ch. VI, p. 115.
55. Codex Mendoza (1979), Third Part, p. 164.
56. Vaillant (1950), p. 115.
57. Soustelle (1980), Ch. V, p. 172.
58. Ibid., p. 170; Sahagún (1829), Vol. II, Bk. VI, Ch. XXXVII.
59. Codex Mendoza, p. 165.
60. Gallenkamp, Ch. 8, p. 148.
61. Landa, Ch. XXXII, p. 58.
62. Morley, Ch. X, p. 208.
63. Ibid., Appendix II, p. 507.
64. Ibid.
65. Ibid.
66. Romé, Ch. 3, p. 28.
67. Von Hagen (1973), Ch. 14, p. 247.
68. Mason, Ch. 9, p. 146.
69. Cieza de León, p. 315.

Chapter VII. The Child

70. Acosta, Bk. VI, Ch. 27, p. 315.
71. Clavijero, Bk. VII, p. 202.
72. Zorita, Ch. IX, p. 63.
73. Ibid.
74. Ibid.
75. Ibid.
76. Vaillant (1950), Ch. VI, p. 116.
77. Clavijero, Bk. VII, p. 202.
78. Peterson, Ch. VI, p. 106.
79. Ibid., p. 116.
80. Ibid.

81. Zorita, Ch. IX, p. 70.
82. Garibay (1963), Ch. 7, p. 140.
83. Ibid., p. 142.
84. Codex Mendoza (1979), Third Part.
85. Vaillant (1950), Ch. VI, p. 116.
86. Landa, Ch. XXX, p. 54.
87. Morley, Ch. X, p. 206.
88. Ibid., p. 208.
89. Ibid., Ch. II, p. 51.
90. Landa, Ch. XXX, p. 54.
91. Ibid., p. 55.
92. Von Hagen (1957), Ch. 9, p. 241.
93. Ibid., p. 245.
94. Ibid., p. 246.
95. Romé, Ch. 3, p. 23.
96. Von Hagen (1957), Ch. 11, p. 436.
97. Guamán Poma de Ayala, Vol. I, pp. 188, 208.
98. Ibid., p. 209.
99. Romé, Ch. 3, p. 23.
100. Guamán Poma de Ayala, p. 207.
101. Romé, Ch. 3, p. 23.
102. Ibid., p. 25.
103. Ibid., p. 25.
104. Mason, Ch. 9, p. 146.
105. Guamán Poma de Ayala, Vol. I, p. 185.
106. Ibid., p. 205.
107. Ibid., p. 203.
108. Ibid., p. 183.
109. Ibid., p. 181.

Chapter VIII. Youth

110. Valliant (1950), Ch. VI, p. 117.
111. Codex Mendoza (1979), Third Part, Folio 61.
112. Torquemada, Vol. III, Bk. IX, Ch. XIII, p. 275.
113. Sahagún (1978), Bk. III, Appendix, p. 56.
114. Peterson, Ch. VI, p. 108.
115. Ibid., p. 109.
116. Ibid.
117. Sahagún (1978), p. 61.
118. Ibid., Ch. 7; Peterson, Ch. VI,

p. 109.

119. Peterson, Ch. VI, p. 110.

120. Ibid.

121. Soustelle (1980), Ch. V, p. 17.

122. Ibid.

123. Sahagún (1978), Bk. VI, Ch. XXXX, p. 215.

124. Soustelle (1980), Ch. V, p. 174.

125. Ibid., p. 175.

126. Ibid.

127. Ibid., p. 176.

128. Garibay (1979), Ch. VII, p. 144.

129. Landa, Ch. XXVI, p. 44.

130. Gallenkamp, Ch. 8, p. 150.

131. Guamán Poma de Ayala, Vol. I, p. 201.

132. Ibid., p. 179.

133. Romé, Ch. 3, p. 28.

134. Mason, Ch. 9, p. 147.

135. Von Hagen (1973), Ch. 14, p. 247.

136. Mason, Ch. 9, p. 147.

137. Prescott (1843), Ch. III, p. 787.

138. Mason, Ch. 12, p. 175.

139. Brundage, Ch. 7, p. 129.

140. Ibid., p. 130.

141. Garcilaso de la Vega, Vol. II, Bk. VIII, p. 252.

142. Prescott (1843), Ch. IV, p. 792.

Chapter IX. Games and Toys

143. Shein, Ch. IV, p. 8.

144. Ibid., p. 10.

145. Ibid., p. 14.

146. Erikson.

147. Hernández (1969), p. 8.

148. Ibid., p. 9.

149. Guamán Poma de Ayala, Vol. I, pp. 180, 184.

150. Siméon, p. 379.

151. Romé, Ch. 12, p. 93.

152. Barrera, p. 12.

153. Siméon, p. 374.

154. Barrera, p. 112.

155. Landa, Ch. XXX, p. 54.

156. Florentine Codex, Bk. VIII, Folio 42 verso.

157. Ibid., Folio 19.

158. Durán, Vol. I, Ch. XXIII, p.202.

159. Piña Chan (1969), p. 14.

160. Díaz del Castillo, Vol. I, Ch. XCVII, p. 356.

161. Piña Chan (1969), p. 33.

162. Barrera, p. 12.

163. Ibid., p. 796.

164. Piña Chan (1969), p. 38.

165. Durán, Vol. I, Ch. XXIII, p. 205.

166. Casas, Section II, Ch. IX, p. 34.

167. Romé, Ch. 12, p. 94.

168. Ibid.

Chapter X. Childhood Diseases and Their Therapy

169. Sahagún (1978), Bk. VI, Ch. XXX.

170. Coury, Ch. XI, p. 176.

171. Sahagún (1978), Bk. X, Ch. VIII.

172. Coury, Ch. XII, p. 190.

173. Ibid., Ch. XI, p. 178.

174. Ibid., Ch. XII, p. 198.

175. Ibid., p. 191.

176. Garcilaso de la Vega, Vol. I, Ch. XXIV, p. 171.

177. Coury, Ch. XII, p. 195.

178. Sahagún (1978), Bk. X, Ch. XXVIII, p. 141.

179. Ibid., p. 145.

180. Ibid.

181. Ibid.

182. Ibid., p. 149.

183. Ibid., pp. 149-50.

184. López Austin, p. 49.

185. Ibid., p. 54.

186. Sahagún (1978), p. 151.

187. Ibid., pp. 151-52.

188. Sahagún (1956), Appendix III, p. 908.

189. Ibid., p. 909.

190. Guerra (1972), Vol. I, p. 308.

191. Ibid., p. 308.

192. Garcilaso de la Vega, Vol. I, Ch. XXIV, p. 172.

193. Guerra (1972), in Laín Entralgo, Vol. I, p. 306.

Chapter XI. Child Sacrifice

194. Sahagún (1829), Vol. I, Bk. II, Ch. XX, p. 82.

195. Sahagún (1978), Bk. II, Ch. 1, pp. 1-2.

196. Ibid., Ch. IV, p. 8.

197. Ibid., Ch. XX, pp. 43-44.

198. Sahagún (1829), Vol. I, Bk. II, Ch. XX, p. 84.

199. Sahagún (1978), Bk. II, Ch. XVIII, p. 34.

200. Ibid., Ch. XXXVIII, pp. 152-53.

201. Casas, Section IV, Ch. XXIV, p. 84.

202. Ibid., Section IV, Ch. XXX, p. 98.

203. Ibid., p. 97.

204. Morley, Ch. XI, p. 288.

205. Landa, Ch. XXVIII, p. 50.

206. Gallenkamp, Ch. 7, p. 134.

207. Ibid., Ch. 12, p. 214.

208. Ibid., p. 218.

209. Ruz, see Bibliography.

210. Guerra (1971), Ch. VII, p. 260.

211. Ibid., Ch. IV, pp. 87, 108.

212. Acosta, Ch. 19, p. 248.

213. Ibid., pp. 249-50.

214. Brundage, Ch. 9, p. 172.

215. Cieza, Ch. 39, p. 127.

216. Mason, Ch. 13, pp. 202-203.

Chapter XII. Ixtlilton the Healer God of Aztec Children

217. Sahagún (1975), Appendix I, p. 888.

218. *Codex Borbonicus*, plate 35.

219. *Codex Borgia*, Vol. I, p. 216.

220. Siméon, p. 232.

221. Sahagún (1829), Vol. I, Bk. I, Ch. XVI, p. 24.

Chapter XIII. Epilogue: The History of Children

222. De Mause, Ch. 1, p. 1.

223. Abt-Garrison, Ch. 1, p. 113.

224. Hogan, see Bibliography.

225. Freud, see Bibliography.

226. Payne, see Bibliography.

227. Ariès, see Bibliography.

228. Abt-Garrison, see Bibliography.

229. Mause, see Bibliography.

230. Hunt, see Bibliography.

231. León-Portilla (1979), Ch. V, pp. 223, 225.

232. León-Portilla (1980), Ch. IX.

233. Ibid., Ch. XIII, p. 305.

234. Lara, Appendix, p. 158.

Appendix A. Superstitions in the Aztec Home

235. Florentine Codex, Vol. I, Bk. V, Appendix, Folio 15.

Appendix B. Aztec Fathers' Advice to their Sons

236. Florentine Codex, Vol. II, Ch. 22, Folio 100.

Appendix C. Aztec Fathers' Advice to their Daughters

237. Florentine Codex, Bk. VI, Ch. 18, Folio 75.

BIBLIOGRAPHY

Abt, Arthur F., *Abt-Garrison: History of Pediatrics.* Philadelphia: W. B. Saunders, 1965.

Acosta, Fray José de, *Historia Natural y Moral de las Indias.* México: Fondo de Cultura Económica, 1940.

Ariès, Philippe, *Centuries of Childhood.* New York: Vintage Books, 1962.

Barrera Vásquez, Alfredo, Ed., *Diccionario Maya Cordemex: Maya-Español, Español-Maya.* Mérida: Ediciones Cordemex, 1980.

Baudot, Georges, *Las Letras Precolombinas.* México: Siglo XXI/América Nuestra, 1979.

Behlmer, George K., *Child Abuse and Moral Reform in England, 1870-1908.* Stanford: Stanford University Press, 1982.

Bernal, Ignacio, "Formación y Desarrollo de Mesoamérica." In *Historia General de México.* México: El Colegio de México, 1976.

—, *A History of Mexican Archaeology: The Vanished Civilizations of Middle America.* London: Thames & Hudson, 1980.

Brundage, Burr C., *Empire of the Inca.* Norman: University of Oklahoma Press, 1963.

Casas, Fray Bartolomé de las, *Los Indios de México y Nueva España.* México: Editorial Porrúa, 1966.

Cieza de León, Pedro de, *The Incas.* Norman: University of Oklahoma Press, 1959.

Clavijero, Francisco Javier, *Historia Antigua de México.* México: Editorial Porrúa, 1968.

Codex Magliabecchi, Zulia Nuttall, Ed. Berkeley: University of California, 1903.

Codex Mendoza: Aztec Manuscript. Freibourg: Productions Liber, 1978.

Códice Borbónico: Manuscrito Mexicano de la Biblioteca del Palais Bourbon: Publicado en facsímil. México: Siglo XXI/América Nuestra, 1979.

Códice Borgia: Edición Facsimilar Comentada por Eduard Seler. México: Fondo de Cultura Económica, 1963.

Códice Florentino: Edición Facsímil, editada por la Secretaría de Gobernación de la República Mexicana y Supervisada por el Archivo General de la Nación. México: 1979.

Códice Mendocino: Edición Facsímil, pátrocinada por la Presidencia de la República. México: San Angel Ediciones, 1979.

Coury, Charles, *La Medicine de l'Amerique Precolombienne.* Paris: Les Editions Roger Dacosta, 1969.

Cruz, Martín de la, *Libellus Medicinalibus Indorum Herbis*, Traducción de Juan Badiano. México: Instituto Mexicano del Seguro Social, 1964.

De Mause, Lloyd, *The History of Childhood.* New York: Psychohistory Press, 1974.

Díaz del Castillo, Bernal, *Historia Verdadera de la Conquista de la Nueva España.* México: Editorial Azteca, 1955.

Diccionario Poliglota Incaico: Compuesto por algunos religiosos franciscanos. Lima: Tipografía de los Colegios de Propaganda Fide del Perú, 1905.

Dubos, René, *Celebrations of Life.* New York: McGraw Hill, 1981.

Durán, Fray Diego, *Historia de las Indias de la Nueva España e Islas de la Tierra Firme.* México: Editorial Porrúa, 1967.

—, *Book of the Gods and Rites* and *The Ancient Calendar.* Norman: University of Oklahoma Press, 1971.

Engel, Frederic André, *An Ancient World Preserved: Relics and Records of Prehistory in the Andes.* New York: Crown, 1976.

Erikson, Erik, *Juego y Desarrollo.* Barcelona: Crítica, 1982.

Freud, Sigmund, *Three Essays on the Theory of Sexuality.* London: Hogarth Press, 1968. Standard Edition, Vol. VII.

Gallenkamp, Charles, *Los Mayas.* México: Editorial Diana, 1981.

Garcilaso de la Vega, ''El Inca,'' *Comentarios Reales.* México: SEP/UNAM, 1982.

Garibay, Angel María, *Epica Náhuatl.* México: UNAM, 1945.

—, *Panorama Literario de los Pueblos Nahuas.* México: Editorial Porrúa, 1963.

Girard, Raphael, *Historia de la Civilizaciones Antiguas de América.* México: Hyspamerica Edición, 1976.

Guamán Poma de Ayala, Felipe, *El Primer Nueva Corónica y Buen Gobierno.* México: Siglo XXI/América Nuestra, 1980.

Guerra, Francisco, *The Precolumbian Mind.* London: Seminar Press, 1971.

—, in Pedro Laín Entralgo, *Historia Universal de la Medicina.* 1972.

Hagen, Victor W. von, *The Ancient Sun Kingdoms of the Americas—Aztec—Maya—Inca.* New York: World Publishing, 1957.

—, *The Ancient Sun Kingdoms of the Americas.* London: Granada Publishing, 1973.

Hernández, Francisco Javier, *El Juguete Popular en México.* México: Ediciones México, Vol. 10, 1950.

—, ''¿Hubo Juguetes en la Epoca Prehispánica?'' *Artes de México*, Año XVI,

No. 125 (1969), p. 5.

Hogan, Louise, *A Study of a Child.* London: Harper & Brothers, 1898.

Hunt, David, *Parents and Children in History.* London: Basic Books, 1970.

Ixtlixochitl, Fernando de Alva, *Obras Históricas.* México: Instituto de Investigaciones Históricas, UNAM, 1975.

Karsh, Estrellita, "Children and Medicine." In *Medical Health Annual.* Chicago: Encyclopedia Britannica, 1980.

Krickeberg, Walter, *Mitos y Leyendas de los Aztecas, Incas, Mayas y Muiscas.* México: Fondo de Cultura Económica, 1980.

Laín Entralgo, Pedro, *Historia Universal de la Medicina.* Barcelona: Salvat Editores, 1972.

Landa, Fray Diego de, *Relación de las Cosas de Yucatán.* México: Editorial Porrúa, 1978.

Lara, Jesús, *La Poesía Quechua.* México: Fondo de Cultura Económica/Tierra Firme, 1979.

Larroyo, Francisco, *Historia Comparada de la Educación en México.* México: Editorial Porrúa, 1952.

Leander, Birgitta, *Flor y Canto: La Poesía de los Aztecas.* México: Instituto Nacional Indigenista/Secretaría de Educación Pública, 1981.

León-Portilla, Miguel, *Los Antiguos Mexicanos.* México: Fondo de Cultura Económica, 1961.

—, *La Filosofía Náhuatl.* México: Instituto de Investigaciones Históricas, UNAM, 1979.

—, *Toltecayotl: Aspectos de la Cultura Náhuatl.* México: Fondo de Cultura Económica, 1980.

López Austin, Alfredo, *Textos de Medicina Náhuatl.* México: Instituto de Investigaciones Históricas, UNAM, 1975.

Lorenzana, Francisco Antonio, *Historia de Nueva España: Edición Facsímile* [Hernán Cortés]. México: Miguel Angel Porrúa, 1980.

Martinez Cortés, Fernando, *Las Ideas en la Medicina Náhuatl.* México: La Prensa Médica Mexicana, 1965.

Mason, J. Alden, *Las Antiguas Culturas del Perú.* México: Fondo de Cultura Económica, 1978.

Molina, Fray Alonso de, *Vocabulario en Lengua Castellana y Mexicana y Mexicana y Castellana.* México: Editorial Porrúa, 1977.

Morley, Sylvanus G., *La Civilización Maya.* México: Fondo de Cultura Económica, 1961.

— and George W. Brainard, *The Ancient Maya,* 4th Ed. Stanford: Stanford University Press, 1983.

Nicolau d'Olwer, Luis, *Cronistas de las Culturas Precolombinas.* México: Fondo de Cultura Económica, 1981.

Padilla Bendezu, Abraham, *Guamán Poma: El Indio Cronista Dibujante.* México: Fondo de Cultura Económica, 1979.

Payne, George Henry, *The Child in Human Progress.* New York: G. P. Putnam's Sons, 1916.

Peterson, Frederick, *Ancient Mexico*. New York: Capricorn Books, 1959.

Piña Chan, Roman, *Mesoamérica—Ensayo Histórico Cultural—Memorias VI*. México: INAH/SEP, 1960.

—, *Games and Sport in Old Mexico*. Leipzig: Edition Leipzig, 1969.

Prescott, William H., *History of the Conquest of Mexico* and *History of the Conquest of Peru*. New York: Random House, 1943.

Romé, Jesús, and Lucienne, *La Vie des Incas dans l'Ancien Perou*. Milan: Editions Minerva, 1978.

Ruz Lhuillier, Alberto, "The Mystery of the Temple of the Inscriptions." *Archaeology*, Vol. 6, No. 1 (1963), pp. 3-11.

Sahagún, Fray Bernardino de, *Historia General de las Cosas de la Nueva España*, Editado por Carlos María Bustamante. México: Imprenta del Ciudadaño Alejandro Valdés, 1829. Collection of Roberto Kerbel.

—, *Historia General de las Cosas de la Nueva España*, Editado por Miguel Acosta Saignes. México: Editorial Alfa, 1955.

—, *Historia General de las Cosas de la Nueva España*, Editado por Angel María Garibay. México: Editorial Porrúa, 1975.

—, *General History of the Things of New Spain*, 2nd Ed. Translated from the Aztec into English, Arthur J. O. Anderson and Charles E. Dibble, Eds. Santa Fe: School of American Research/University of Utah, 1978.

Séjourné, Laurette, *Supervivencias de un Mundo Mágico*, Debujos de Leonora Carrington. México: Fondo de Cultura Económica/Tezontle, 1953.

Shein, Rosa Korbman de, *El Juego como Método Diagnóstico en Psicología Infantil*. México: Facultad de Filosofia y Letras, UNAM, 1963.

Siméon, Rémi, Ed., *Diccionario de la Lengua Náhuatl o Mexicana*. México: Siglo XXI, 1981.

Solís, Antonio de, *Historia de la Conquista de México*. Seville: 1735. Collection of the author.

Soustelle, Jacques, *La Vie Quotidienne des Aztèques à la Veille de la Conquête Espagnole*. Paris: Librairie Hachette, 1955.

—, *Daily Life of the Aztecs on the Eve of the Spanish Conquest*. Stanford: Stanford University Press, 1961.

—, *La vida Cotidiana de los Aztecas*. México: Fondo de Cultura Económica, 1980.

Stark, Louise R., Ed., *Diccionario Español-Quichua-Quichua-Español*. Ecuador: Editorial Banco Central de Ecuador, 1977.

Torquemada, Fray Juan de, *Monarquía Indiana*. México: Instituto de Investigaciones Históricas, UNAM, 1975.

Vaillant, George C., *The Aztecs of Mexico: Origin, Rise and Fall of the Aztec Nation*. Harmondsworth: Penguin Books, 1956.

Whitlock, Ralph, *Everyday Life of the Maya*. London: B. T. Batsford, 1976.

Zorita, Alonso de, *Los Señores de la Nueva España*. México: Imprenta Universitaria, 1942.

INDEX

The author is a practicing pediatrician and a resident of
Mexico City. He has been director of a children's hospi-
tal and teaches pediatrics at the university level in Mexico and Israel. Dr. Shein is a member of several professional medical organizations and also of the Instituto
Mexicano de Cultura; he is president-elect of the Mexican Society of History and Philosophy of Medicine and
is the author and translator of several works on pediatrics and childhood.

Artist Jorge Flores also lives and works in Mexico but
has exhibited widely. He has studied precolumbian art
forms and has added Mexican ethnicity and history to his
themes. Working with muralist David Alfaro Siqueiros
and independently he has produced a number of monu-
mental creations.